Toy Makers

Other books in the History Makers series:

Ancient Philosophers

Artists of the Renaissance

Astronauts

Baseball Greats

Cartoonists

Civil War Generals of the Confederacy

Civil War Generals of the Union

Cult Leaders

Dictators

Disease Detectives

Fighters Against American Slavery

Fighters Against Censorship

Gangsters

Great Authors of Children's Literature

Great Composers

Great Conquerors

Great Male Comedians

Great Women Comedians

Gunfighters

Heroes of the Holocaust

Hitler's Henchmen

Home Run Kings

Influential First Ladies

The Kennedys

Leaders of Black Civil Rights

Leaders of Women's Suffrage

Legendary Football Quarterbacks

Magicians and Illusionists

Male Olympic Champions

Medieval Knights and Warriors

Native American Chiefs and Warriors

Pioneers of the American West

Pioneers of the Internet

Pirates

Polar Explorers

Presidential Assassins

Presidents and Scandals

Rock and Roll Legends

Rulers of Ancient Egypt

Scientists of Ancient Greece

Serial Killers

Spies

Twentieth-Century American Writers

Women Inventors

Women Leaders of Nations

Women of the American Revolution

Women Olympic Champions

Women Pop Stars

History MAKERS

Toy Makers

By Linda Skeers

**LUCENT
BOOKS**®

THOMSON

GALE

San Diego • Detroit • New York • San Francisco • Cleveland
New Haven, Conn. • Waterville, Maine • London • Munich

LIBRARY OF CONGRESS CATALOGING-IN-PUBLICATION DATA

Skeers, Linda.
 Toy makers / by Linda Skeers.
  p. cm. — (History makers)
 Includes bibliographical references and index.
 Summary: Profiles the lives of several legendary toy makers and the toys they created,
 including Milton Bradley, Ole Kirk Christiansen, and Joshua Lionel Cowen of "Lionel" Trains.
  ISBN 1-59018-336-3
  1. Toy makers—Biography. I. Title. II. Series.
  TS2301.T7S57 2004
  338.7'68872'092273—dc21
                                                                    2003006840

Printed in the United States of America

CONTENTS

FOREWORD   6

INTRODUCTION
A Tale of Toy Makers   8

CHAPTER 1
Milton Bradley: Game Master   11

CHAPTER 2
Joshua Lionel Cowen: A Passion for Trains   25

CHAPTER 3
Alfred Carlton Gilbert: Making Science Fun   38

CHAPTER 4
Ole Kirk Christiansen: LEGO Brick Builder   51

CHAPTER 5
Ruth Handler: Barbie and Mattel's Matriarch   67

CHAPTER 6
Lonnie G. Johnson: Super Soaker Inventor   81

Notes   95
For Further Reading   99
Works Consulted   101
Index   105
Picture Credits   111
About the Author   112

FOREWORD

The literary form most often referred to as "multiple biography" was perfected in the first century A.D. by Plutarch, a perceptive and talented moralist and historian who hailed from the small town of Chaeronea in central Greece. His most famous work, *Parallel Lives*, consists of a long series of biographies of noteworthy ancient Greek and Roman statesmen and military leaders. Frequently, Plutarch compares a famous Greek to a famous Roman, pointing out similarities in personality and achievements. These expertly constructed and very readable tracts provided later historians and others, including playwrights like Shakespeare, with priceless information about prominent ancient personages and also inspired new generations of writers to tackle the multiple biography genre.

The Lucent History Makers series proudly carries on the venerable tradition handed down from Plutarch. Each volume in the series consists of a set of five to eight biographies of important and influential historical figures who were linked together by a common factor. In *Rulers of Ancient Rome*, for example, all the figures were generals, consuls, or emperors of either the Roman Republic or Empire; while the subjects of *Fighters Against American Slavery*, though they lived in different places and times, all shared the same goal, namely, the eradication of human servitude. Mindful that politicians and military leaders are not (and never have been) the only people who shape the course of history, the editors of the series have also included representatives from a wide range of endeavors, including scientists, artists, writers, philosophers, religious leaders, and sports figures.

Each book is intended to give a range of figures—some well known, others less known; some who made a great impact on history, others who made only a small impact. For instance, by making Columbus's initial voyage possible, Spain's Queen Isabella I, featured in *Women Leaders of Nations*, helped to open up the New World to exploration and exploitation by the European powers. Inarguably, therefore, she made a major contribution to a series of events that had momentous consequences for the entire world. By contrast, Catherine II, the eighteenth-century Russian queen, and Golda Meir, the modern Israeli prime minister, did not play roles of global impact; however, their policies and actions significantly influenced the historical development of both their own countries and their regional neighbors. Regardless of their relative importance in the greater historical scheme, all of the figures chronicled in the History Makers series made contributions to posterity; and their public achievements, as well as what is known about their private lives, are presented and evaluated in light of the most recent scholarship.

In addition, each volume in the series is documented and substantiated by a wide array of primary and secondary source quotations. The primary source quotes enliven the text by presenting eyewitness views of the times and culture in which each history maker lived, while the secondary source quotes, taken from the works of respected modern scholars, offer expert elaboration and/ or critical commentary. Each quote is footnoted, demonstrating to the reader exactly where biographers find their information. The footnotes also provide the reader with the means of conducting additional research. Finally, to further guide and illuminate readers, each volume in the series features photographs, two bibliographies, and a comprehensive index.

The History Makers series provides both students engaged in research and more casual readers with informative, enlightening, and entertaining overviews of individuals from a variety of circumstances, professions, and backgrounds. No doubt all of them, whether loved or hated, benevolent or cruel, constructive or destructive, will remain endlessly fascinating to each new generation seeking to identify the forces that shaped their world.

A Tale of Toy Makers

The first toys were often made for children by their relatives; sometimes a kindly grandfather carved a wooden horse, or a mother shaped a cornhusk into a doll for her daughter. Children made many of their own playthings, too. Toys were fashioned by whatever was at hand. The metal hoop from a broken wooden barrel, discarded horseshoes, odd-shaped stones, and bits of string and cloth scraps were made into toys.

For children long ago, having time to play with toys was rare. Children spent their days doing chores to help the family. They took care of the garden, tended the farm animals, picked fruits and berries, watched their younger siblings, and gathered firewood. In some regions, children often toiled long hours in the fields or worked in factories or mines. Taking time to play was considered unimportant and unnecessary.

Over time, society's attitude toward leisure activities changed. Milton Bradley, the man behind some of the world's most beloved board games, strived to educate the public in the importance of families spending time together—just having fun. He believed that children should not be viewed as small adults but as separate, growing, inquisitive beings. Bradley helped parents realize that toys were an important part of a child's educational process.

As more people accepted these ideas, toy making as an industry slowly began to take shape. Fewer toys were handmade from crude and simple designs. In 1785, an advertisement appeared in the *Independent Gazetteer* featuring mass-produced toys for sale. By the early 1800s, tinsmiths had invented simple machines that could produce tin toys faster than by crafting them by hand. These toys were stocked in dry goods stores or sold by peddlers who traveled in wagons.

Toy making as a profession was attractive to artisans, woodcarvers, and entrepreneurs. As Elliot Handler, cofounder of Mattel, said in a speech, "From its beginning around 1840, the American toy industry was a place where a man with an idea, craftmanship and the desire to succeed had a pretty good chance of getting started."[1]

That desire to succeed played an enormous part in the lives of the toy makers profiled here. Ruth Handler's own company rejected her idea for Barbie several times before the teenage fashion doll became a reality. It took Lonnie G. Johnson eight years to interest a company in his Super Soaker. These toy makers all believed in their creation and were determined to see it succeed, despite the odds stacked against them.

Although these toy makers all lived at different times and created different toys, they each had an indomitable spirit that allowed them to pursue their dream no matter what obstacles and challenges they faced along the way. Some faced financial difficulties; others had to overcome personal tragedies. The path to success was not easy for any of them.

Three kids race their toy car down the street. Toy makers recognize that playtime is an important part of a child's development.

Another quality these toy makers share is originality. Many toy fads and crazes are best-sellers one year and overflowing the sale bins or popping up at garage sales the next. A great toy that can stand the test of time educates, stimulates the child's own imagination and creativity, and provides endless hours of fun and enjoyment.

A truly gifted toy maker always keeps in mind the needs of a child. These toy makers succeeded where so many others failed because they observed children and allowed them to test products throughout the toy-making process, from the initial idea to the finished product.

Toy making is now a serious business. Toys and games are no longer considered a frivolous luxury but an important part of our society and culture. As author and avid toy collector Harry L. Rinker explains, "Toys play many roles: expanding one's imagination, understanding the simple pleasures of fun, enhancing deductive powers, and teaching the joy of victory and the agony of defeat."[2] Great toy makers understand that philosophy and create toys that encompass many, if not all, of those traits.

This is a group of unique individuals with a variety of backgrounds from rocket scientist to magician, from carpenter to printer. Despite their differences, they all succeeded in a difficult industry. They not only created some of the most beloved and cherished toys, but also helped change the way society viewed children and playtime. Their fierce determination, perseverance in the face of adversity, creativity, and insight into children made them all truly legendary in the toy industry.

CHAPTER 1

Milton Bradley: Game Master

Milton Bradley was born November 8, 1836, in Vienna, Maine. He was the only child of Lewis and Fannie Lyford Bradley. Lewis had a knack for fixing things but could not support his family on a handyman's meager wages. The three of them moved frequently as Lewis Bradley sought employment. Instead of having a negative effect on young Bradley, the tough times and frequent moves brought the family closer.

Early Days

The Bradleys doted on Milton and held the view that feeding a young mind was as important as feeding a young body. As a result, they were actively involved in his education. When Milton was six he struggled to understand addition, so his father placed six shiny red apples in front of him. Milton could count the six apples but could not understand *why* four apples plus two apples added up to six apples.

His father patiently took two apples off the table. Milton counted them again and realized that numbers represented *things*. His success was celebrated by chomping into an apple. From that moment on, he had a love and appreciation for math and knew that learning could be fun.

Often, the Bradleys played strategic games like chess and checkers from homemade sets. They also read and discussed books—from the Bible to Shakespeare. Milton's parents included him in their discussions on current issues. Learning, debating, and exploring new ideas were intertwined with leisure and fun in the Bradley family. It was a philosophy Bradley adhered to for the rest of his life.

An Uneven Path

Milton Bradley's road to success as a toy maker was rocky. He had a series of jobs while in high school—sweeping floors, delivering goods, and clerking in a dry goods store. In 1854, after graduating from high school, Bradley worked for Oliver E. Cushman, a draftsman and patent agent, where he had hands-on training in mechanical drafting. His spare time was spent selling stationery supplies. He knew the best time to approach potential customers was right after they were paid. As he explains,

> As a certain portion of the corporations paid off each week, I always selected the days when the girls were "flush" [just received cash]. . . . I, in fact, had an *established* trade which competitors who learned my methods tried in vain to take from me, as the girls would wait for me.[3]

Despite his success, Bradley was not satisfied with being a salesman. He yearned for a job that would combine two of his favorite things—math and drawing.

In June 1856, Bradley was looking for work as a draftsman, although he had little practical work experience to recommend him to an employer. He boldly entered the Wason Car–Manufacturing Company and told the owner he should hire him as a draftsman. The owner looked over the young man and said that if he could draw a locomotive, he would be hired.

Bradley agreed, though he had never before drawn a locomotive. He studied the sketches around the room and began scratching out a locomotive in a piece of wood. After completing it, he was hired, earning $1.25 per day. Unfortunately, in 1858, the company went out of business. Once again, Bradley found himself wandering the streets looking for work.

Open for Business

At that time, the country was caught up in a spirit of creativity and optimism. The cotton gin, steam engine, and mortised lock were new inventions. The United States Patent Office had opened in 1836, and people needed scientific drawings of their inventions if they hoped to profit from their ideas. Bradley saw an opportunity to go into business as a draftsman and do the complex mechanical drawings needed to secure a patent.

Bradley rented a small office on the upper floor of 247 Main Street. On a September morning in 1858, he proudly hung the gilt sign he had lettered himself proclaiming MILTON BRADLEY— Mechanical Draftsman and Patent Solicitor.

Author James J. Shea describes the first day of Bradley's venture: "Opening the door, he stepped inside and smiled at his new drawing board, his rolltop desk, filing cabinet and two chairs which he'd bought with his savings. Then he stretched out in a chair and waited for the business to begin. He waited . . . and he waited."[4]

Famed board game maker Milton Bradley began his career as a draftsman and printer.

Lithography

Bradley needed a second income. He accepted a unique assignment from T.W. Wason & Company, a branch of the previous company he had worked for. Bradley would do mechanical drawings of an elaborate $10,000 railroad car for the pasha of Egypt. After working day and night to complete the drawings for the three apartments and two drawing rooms of the car, he earned enough money to buy a diamond ring for his fiancée, Vilona Eaton.

Pleased with his work, the company presented Bradley with a colored lithograph of the palatial railroad car. Bradley proudly hung it over his desk, staring at it often. He was not interested in locomotives but in lithography, an interest he decided to pursue.

Pictured is an advertisement for Bradley's lithography business. The venture failed, however, and Bradley soon turned to printing.

In January 1860, Bradley bought a lithographic press from a firm in Providence, Rhode Island, and spent two weeks learning to operate it. The press was shipped to Springfield, Massachusetts, and he opened up a new business. The old sign was removed and a new one hung:

MILTON BRADLEY CO.

Publishers

Lithographers

Bradley had not comprehended how painstakingly precise lithography was. Additionally, with only one other press in New England, hiring experienced printers was impossible. His lithography business failed to thrive, so he shifted his focus to printing.

Playing for Keeps

In the summer of 1860, Bradley's old schoolmate and friend George Tapley invited him to spend an evening playing a board game.

Bradley had been depressed about his idle press and looked forward to the diversion. They played an old English board game in which opponents moved oval discs around the board.

Not everyone considered game playing an acceptable pastime. Many people, especially those with Puritan beliefs, felt games of chance were sinful and that idle hours should be spent in higher pursuits. As Bradley moved the discs around the board, he remembered how much fun he had playing chess and checkers with his father. What if he combined fun along with good moral values in his own board game?

Bradley divided a square board into eighty-four spaces. Red squares would be neutral, while white squares would represent values. According to author Bruce Whitehill, "Landing on Bravery sent the player to Honor, Perseverance to Success, and Ambition to Fame. Gambling led to Ruin, and Idleness to Disgrace." [5] Winners made it to Happy Old Age, while losers landed in Ruin. Studying the checkered pattern of the board reminded him of how life was checkered with challenges, decisions, and rewards. He called his creation The Checkered Game of Life. He would use his press to print the game himself. There was no technology to mass-produce games at the time, so Bradley and one assistant cut and packaged the board games themselves.

With samples of his game, Bradley traveled to New York and recited his speech in the first stationery store to which he came:

> I have come to New York with some samples of a new and most amazing game, sir. A highly moral game, may I say, that encourages children to lead exemplary lives and entertains both old and young with the spirit of its friendly competition. [6]

After two days, Bradley had sold all his games to news vendors, department stores, and stationery stores. Confident of his business success and ability to support a family, Bradley married Vilona Eaton on his twenty-fourth birthday, November 8, 1860. He could have continued producing board games, but his sense of duty to his country intervened.

Lincoln's Whiskers

Bradley was asked by Admiral Samuel Bowles, a delegate to the Republican National Convention, to produce and sell photos of the Republican nominee for president, a young, clean-shaven politician named Abraham Lincoln. Since Bradley supported Lincoln's abolitionist ideology, he immediately stopped printing The Checkered Game of Life and concentrated on Lincoln's photos.

Bradley had not gambled on the influence of eleven-year-old Grace Bedell, who almost destroyed his lithography business. On October 16, 1860, Bedell wrote to Lincoln about his appearance, pointing out, "All the ladies like whiskers and [if you grew a beard] they would tease their husband's to vote for you and then you would be President."[7] Lincoln took her advice and grew a beard. Since Bradley's pictures of a clean-shaven nominee were out-of-date, he destroyed the unwanted pictures. Bradley had stopped printing games and now had no goods to sell.

A New Attitude

With his focus back on The Checkered Game of Life, Bradley confronted the Puritan view of game playing as sinful behavior. He championed the idea that home amusements were *positive* and would help children develop strong moral and ethical characters. As author Bruce Whitehill explains, "Because of the religious and moral fervor during the mid-1800s, gambling was frowned upon and the dice so often associated with gambling games were considered 'tools of the devil.'"[8] To counter this, Bradley had players spin a teetotum, similar to a top with numbers on the side.

He started printing and successfully selling The Checkered Game of Life again. Whitehill believes its acceptance can be attributed to its underlying morals. He explains the game's purpose: "While furnishing amusement it was supposed to indicate the idea that good deeds brought rewards and bad deeds trouble."[9]

Patriotic games were popular during the Civil War. After the war, four games were packaged together, labeled The Union Games, and sold for one dollar. The Milton Bradley Company kept the marketing strategy of combining games after their initial peak in sales—when new games appeared, older games were sold in sets of four, prolonging their life in sales.

Children were not the only ones in need of amusement. Bradley frequently passed groups of weary Civil War soldiers warming themselves around fires. Convinced that games would lift their spirits and provide a healthy distraction, he set to work. Bradley produced a lightweight, pocket-sized kit he called Games for the Soldiers. It contained pieces needed to play nine games. At first, he gave them away to soldiers, but within weeks he was bombarded with requests for the first-of-a-kind kits, and it turned into a money-making opportunity. Bradley hired a few more assistants to keep up with the demand for his games.

The public responded to Bradley's patriotic mission to aid soldiers and his campaign to share his values with children. Slowly the perception of game playing became more positive. As sales grew, so

Lincoln grew his trademark beard early in the presidental campaign, and the photos that Bradley took of a clean-shaven Abraham Lincoln became worthless.

did Bradley's company. In 1864, he moved to a larger location and hired more workers. He also took in two business partners who would look after the administrative side of the business while he focused on the creative side.

Croquet Rolls Across the Country

In 1865, croquet fever swept the country. It was played at summer parties on huge estates and in modest backyards. Bradley became interested in croquet when two friends got into a heated argument over the rules. He was intrigued by a lawn game that provoked such strong emotions in the players. Bradley discovered that there was not one uniform set of rules and that croquet sets were flimsy and homemade. He made his own set and played every evening until dark, perfecting the rules.

On April 18, 1866, Bradley's version of croquet was patented. He was the first to mass-produce and sell croquet sets. Each set included his printed rules of the game. The Milton Bradley Company could not keep up with the demand for croquet sets because of a shortage of available wood, so Bradley built a sawmill in Vermont to directly supply his company with the necessary wood. Bradley's father later took charge of the sawmill's operations.

Croquet was considered a pastime for adults, but Bradley realized children were also fascinated by it. He began producing an inexpensive smaller set called Bradley's Popular Croquet. He believed referring to it as the "children's version" made it seem inferior and would hurt children's feelings.

It was often remarked that nearly every family in America owned a croquet set. With that success, Bradley needed something new to offer the public. He puzzled over what would capture their attention. And a puzzle was the answer.

Puzzling Puzzle

In 1867, America was swept up in the frenzy of Bradley's The Terrible Fifteen Puzzle. (Bradley later changed its name to The Mystic Fifteen Puzzle after deciding that the word "terrible" would not successfully

Civil War soldiers pass the time playing cards in camp. Bradley produced a series of games to entertain Union soldiers during the war.

Bradley sits at his desk in his office at the Milton Bradley Company. Bradley hired partners to administer the business while he focused on creating new products.

promote it.) It was a simple yet aggravating handheld puzzle. In a small wooden-framed box were fifteen sliding tiles—in a space designed to hold sixteen tiles. The object was to slide the numbered tiles until they lined up from one to fifteen.

A New York banker became so frustrated with the puzzle that he tossed it overboard from the ferry he was riding. He then changed his mind and wanted to dive in after it. The puzzle was solved first by a newsboy in Boston who was hailed as a genius.

As fast as the tile puzzle fad began, it ended. Bradley concluded that after the Boston newsboy solved it, the puzzle no longer offered a challenge. He vowed to keep challenging the public.

Tough Times for Toy Makers

The Milton Bradley Company struggled during the late 1860s. The country's economy was in a depression. Jobs were scarce, money was tight, and people had to cut back on spending. Bradley knew that the only way he could stay in business was to keep offering new and creative games, puzzles, and amusements—things people simply could not resist. Bradley believed they needed a diversion from the economic hardships of the day.

In 1866, Bradley was rummaging through a box of toys from Germany. A simple tin drum with a series of pictures painted around the outside caught his eye. As he twirled the drum in his hands, Bradley was struck by the notion that the pictures told a story as they rolled by.

Bradley used his press to print a colorful picture story on a long roll of paper. He then rolled the paper inside a large drum with a crank attached. As the crank turned, the story rolled by. Bradley called his creation the Myrioptican. For his first story he drew Civil War scenes and wrote a narrator's script to accompany the pictures. It began:

> Ladies and gentlemen, I have the pleasure to present to you the Myrioptican, which is one of the most interesting and instructive exhibitions that has ever been presented to the public. Our first scene represents Major Anderson and his band of about eighty men, as they appeared on the night of December 26th, 1860, entering Fort Sumter in Charleston Harbor after evacuating Fort Moultrie. [10]

People were mesmerized. Financially it was a success, but Bradley was not satisfied. He believed it was a crude version of his concept and wanted to improve it. He wanted *motion*.

Seeing Is Believing

Bradley was not the only one fascinated by optical illusions and the movement of objects. People had studied the subject for years. He immersed himself in all the scientific and academic studies done previously and experimented with screens, drawings, lanterns, shadows, and drums. An invention called the Zoetrope interested him.

Bradley, seeing its potential, became the first person to manufacture the Zoetrope as a toy. It consisted of a twelve-inch drum with vertical slits cut into its circumference at regular intervals. A strip of drawings—each slightly different to simulate movement—was spaced inside the drum. The drum was attached to a spindle so it could turn easily. When a child looked through the slits while the drum was twirling, the figures appeared to move.

The first Zoetropes were sold with drawings of woodchoppers, rope jumpers, a hurdle race, and a trapeze artist. They sold for $2.50. Bradley had succeeded in creating the first moving picture machine twenty years before Thomas Edison and George Eastman would improve upon the idea.

The Milton Bradley Company was in fine shape, creating board games derived from parlor games such as Aunt Hulda's Courtship. In both the original and Bradley's version, a narrator recites a story and players read from cards to fill in gaps in the story.

After an evening of parlor games, Bradley realized Vilona had not participated as enthusiastically as usual. Throughout the winter she grew weaker and died on March 13, 1867. The lonely, grief-stricken

Bradley asked his parents to move in with him. Once again, the threesome comforted and entertained each other. During this time, Bradley thought about how his parents' views on education differed from society's, and he began reflecting on his other passion, education.

An Interest in Early Education

Bradley was grateful that his parents took an unconventional approach to his education. He was disheartened when he realized that primary schoolchildren in the 1860s learned by repetition and were often whacked on the knuckles with wooden rulers if they did not recite answers correctly.

Bradley may not have acted upon his concerns if he had not met Professor Edward Wiebe in 1868. Wiebe was interested in how children learned. He knew Bradley was interested in education and was a printer by trade, so he asked him to publish a book by Friedrich Wilhelm August Froebel. Unfamiliar with Froebel and his beliefs, Bradley politely declined.

The subject was brought to Bradley's attention again one summer evening in 1869 when he heard Miss Elizabeth Peabody lecture on her educational ideas. She was a teacher, writer, and headmistress of a famous kindergarten in Boston. Miss Peabody was a dynamic speaker, and Bradley was quickly caught up in her enthusiasm, as one observer noted: "And the things she said that evening gripped Milton Bradley as if he'd been cast under a spell." [11]

Miss Peabody spoke eloquently about Froebel's methods. Froebel believed that if children *enjoyed* learning, they would become better students. One key aspect was to incorporate objects—colorful blocks and balls—to help children understand difficult concepts. Bradley remembered his father using apples to

This brochure advertises Bradley's Zoetrope, a device that used moving pictures.

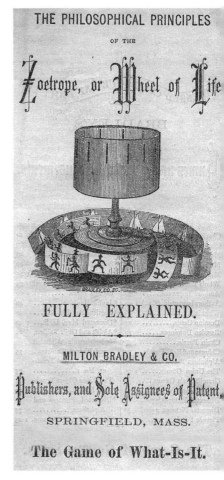

THE PHILOSOPHICAL PRINCIPLES

OF THE

Zoetrope, or Wheel of Life

FULLY EXPLAINED.

MILTON BRADLEY & CO.

Publishers, and Sole Assignees of Patent,

SPRINGFIELD, MASS.

The Game of What-Is-It.

teach him addition. The underlying theme of Froebel's message struck a chord within Bradley.

Improving Kindergarten

After Miss Peabody's lecture, Bradley sought out Professor Wiebe and agreed to publish the manuscript. That fall the Milton Bradley Company published *Paradise of Childhood: A Practical Guide to Kindergartners*. It was the first educational guide of its kind to be published in English. Sales were slow at first, but a few years later the book won a bronze medal at the Philadelphia Exposition of 1876. The book never made a profit for the company, but Bradley believed it was worthwhile and continued printing and distributing it at a financial loss.

Bradley did not stop with one book on education, but also manufactured school equipment, multiplication sticks, rulers, and stencils. He purchased the *Kindergarten News,* a small monthly magazine for teachers. A subscription cost fifty cents per year. He added more articles by prominent educators and writers and renamed it *Kindergarten Review.*

Education, not making money, was Bradley's goal. If schools or teachers needed it, he provided it. As Henry Turner Bailey recounts in a tribute to Bradley,

> To Milton Bradley more than to any other one man is due the success of the kindergarten in the United States, for he spent a fortune in perfecting and distributing the materials required, before the existence of any widespread demand for them. By the excellence of his work and his enthusiasm he helped to create the demand. [12]

Later Years

Bradley's interest in education brought him out of his depression. Once again he began spending time with George Tapley, playing parlor games. During one such evening, he met Ellen (Nellie) Thayer. Courtship followed, with the two of them frequently playing croquet together. They were married on May 21, 1869, and later had two daughters, Florence and Lillian. Bradley's interest in education continued through the 1880s, during which time he wrote a manual called *Help for Ungraded Schools* with tips for rural teachers. His company continued to create and manufacture games and amusements. Bradley paid close attention to popular trends in entertainment. For example, while Buffalo Bill's Wild West Show swept the

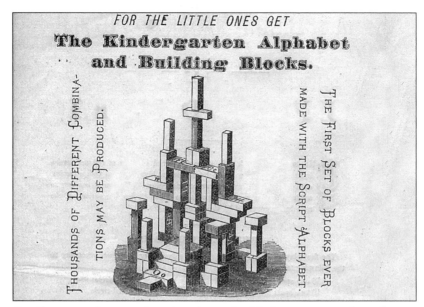

Bradley created many educational toys for kindergartners such as the one shown in this advertisement.

country, the Milton Bradley Company capitalized on that fascination and introduced a wooden Buffalo Bill gun. It sold out as soon as it was introduced in 1884. Inventions of the 1900s inspired new games such as Ring Off—A Wireless Telephone Game, one about car ownership and travel called Auto Game, and another based on airships called Air King.

In 1889, the Bradleys moved to a larger house that was perfect for parties and parlor games. In fact, many board games got their start in Bradley's parlor, since he encouraged any guest with an idea for a new game to visit his office the morning after his parties. One of the most popular of these parlor games was Kerion, in which players race their men around a board, leaping over their opponents to be the first one with all their pieces safely back in their original places.

In 1907, Bradley retired due to poor health. He bought a cottage in Maine, where he liked to hike among the trees, paint watercolors, and go sailing. On a Saturday afternoon in May 1911, Milton and Nellie took a car ride around Springfield and watched children playing croquet on the grass. He died two days later. George Tapley, his friend, schoolmate, and mentor, took over the running of his company.

Life remains a popular board game and is produced in twenty languages and played around the world. It is part of the permanent collection of the Smithsonian's Natural Museum of American History.

Milton Bradley's Twister became popular in the 1960s and remains so today. Although many of the company's most popular games were developed after Bradley's death, each was designed to conform to his high standards.

Other classic Milton Bradley games include Monopoly, Chutes and Ladders, Candyland, Operation, and Battleship, all developed after his death but with his ideals of competition, fairness, education, and fun in mind.

Bradley will be remembered for more than his board games. He changed the way society viewed game playing and devoted himself fully to the process of early education. His contribution to society, and his legacy, live on.

24

CHAPTER 2

Joshua Lionel Cowen: A Passion for Trains

Joshua Lionel Cohen (later Cowen) was born August 25, 1877. He was the eighth of Hyman and Rebecca Cohen's nine children. His parents were Eastern European Jews who immigrated to the United States and settled in New York shortly after the Civil War.

Hyman was in a better position than most immigrants. He spoke English, had enough money to start a business, and knew a trade. He opened a fashionable hatmaker's shop, and the family, while not wealthy, lived comfortably and prospered.

A Curious Kid

Joshua Cowen had an insatiable curiosity, which frequently landed him in trouble. When he wanted to know how the eyes in his sister's delicate porcelain doll's head rolled back and forth, he cracked open the doll's head to see the mechanism for himself.

As a young boy Cowen loved to experiment and invent gadgets. He also had a passion for trains. When he was seven years old, Cowen combined these interests—with disastrous results. He carved a crude locomotive out of wood and put in a small steam engine he had been working on. Unfortunately, the train exploded and set the kitchen curtains and wallpaper on fire. Whatever punishment he received from his parents was not harsh enough to keep him from further inventing.

School Days

Although he loved learning and experimenting with new ideas, Cowen did not like school. He was not an attentive student, quickly became restless and bored in the classroom. When he was twelve years old, his family moved to 104th Street and Madison Avenue, which at that time was a rural area. He often skipped school to watch the trains rattle and whistle down the nearby tracks. He also liked to bicycle around the neighborhood and play baseball in the street with his friends. Cowen belonged to a local hiking group—the Fifty Mile Club—and spent as much time as possible outdoors.

Although he was never a serious student, his parents expected him to go to college and learn a trade. He enrolled in the Peter Cooper Institute high school. It was not long before he lost interest in his studies. The only subject that caught his attention was shop class, where he spent long hours hunched over a workbench working on different projects.

Teenage Tinkerer

Cowen spent his teen years experimenting, inventing, and tinkering—with mixed results. While still in school he designed and built what may have been the very first doorbell using storage batteries for power. His teacher believed it was a worthless invention and "advised him nothing would ever replace the knuckles for announcing one's arrival." [13] Cowen took that advice to heart and moved on to other ideas.

In 1893, at sixteen, Cowen had done well enough in his technical classes to enter the College of the City of New York. He dropped out soon after and took a job at the Acme Electric Lamp Company assembling battery powered lamps. Although his parents disagreed, he felt the hands-on experience he received was more valuable to him than a college degree.

Cowen often experimented with batteries and stayed at work long after his shift was over. He created another unique gadget by sliding thin batteries into a tube that had a small lightbulb on one end. The tube was stuck in a flowerpot and hidden among the leaves, illuminating the plant. Again, this was not the invention that made Cowen a household name, as author Joseph Fucini explains:

> Cowen sold the rights to his invention to a restaurateur named Conrad Hubert, who tried marketing it as a decorative object. After failing to generate much interest in the unusual flowerpot, Hubert decided to detach the tubes and sell them on their own illuminatory merit. Calling his revised product the Eveready Flashlight, he became a multimillionaire. [14]

Although he received none of the profits, Cowen did not regret his decision to sell his rights to the invention. First, financial gain was not his goal. Cowen wanted to create, invent, and push the boundaries of knowledge of power sources. In addition, he did not believe in wasting time dwelling on the past. Cowen's frequently spoken motto was, "To stand still is to move backward!" [15]

Cowen was granted his first patent on November 7, 1899, when he created a photographer's flashlamp that quickly ignited a small amount of flash powder when a photo was taken. It sped up the photography process and resulted in clearer, less blurry photos. Next he developed an explosive fuse that could detonate mines, for which he received a patent on November 13, 1900. Although Cowen sold this device to the United States Navy for twelve thousand dollars, he was not interested in designing more military equipment. Cowen now had enough money to start his own business.

Lionel Manufacturing

Only twenty-three years old, he joined forces with his friend Harry C. Grant to form the Lionel Manufacturing Company. When asked years later why he chose his middle name for the company, he replied, "Well, I had to name it something!" [16]

Their first project was a small portable fan for which Cowen held the patent. Almost immediately the infant company was in trouble, as Cowen explains: "It was the most beautiful thing you ever saw.

Joshua Lionel Cowen (right) demonstrates his electric train to a young fan in 1953. The Lionel name is synonymous with toy trains.

It ran like a dream and it only had one thing wrong with it. You could stand a foot away from the thing and not feel any breeze." [17] Sales of the fan were dismal. The fledging inventor needed a new idea if he was going to stay in business.

Cowen had never forgotten his fascination with trains or his unsuccessful attempt to build a steam-powered locomotive when he was a child. He decided to combine his love of gadgets with his love of trains. He discovered that the fan's small motor was strong enough to propel a wooden railroad car. Cowen and his partner were in business.

A Train's Many Tasks

Cowen did not have children in mind when he built his first train, as he explains: "I sold my first railroad car not as a toy, mind you, but as something to attract attention." [18] And attract attention it did. He called his creation "Miniature Electric Cars . . . For Window Display." In 1902, Cowen convinced Robert Ingersoll, a Manhattan toy store owner, to set up a train display in his store window. The train car was an open rectangular box propelled by his tiny battery powered motor. *Electric Express* was printed in gold letters along the side. The train traveled a circular track carrying toys the storekeeper wanted to feature for a quick sale. The next day Ingersoll ordered more trains. The advertising display itself proved to be more popular with customers than the toys it featured.

Trains were not the only thing on Cowen's mind. In 1902, he met a secretary named Cecelia Liberman on a Manhattan trolley. The two began dating, and Cowen frequently sent Liberman postcards as he traveled the country selling train displays. Two years later, they married, and they later had two children, Lawrence and Isabel. As a young boy, Lawrence's photo often appeared in Lionel ads and on boxes of Lionel trains. Lionel trains were not used only as toy store displays; several restaurant owners saw electric trains as a unique gimmick to draw in customers. Train tracks were set up on lunch counters, and trains would carry plates of food to the amused customers. Who needed a waitress when you had the Luncheon Express?

One Lionel train was set up in New York's Pennsylvania Station to help raise money for charity. Coins dropped into the train car would travel down the track, deposit them into a collection box, and then chug back down the track for more donations.

His Own Path

When Cowen first manufactured miniature trains, he did not view them as toys to be played with by children. However, children were fascinated by trains and in the early 1900s, Cowen realized the potential in marketing them as toys. Europe, especially Germany, had dominated the toy train industry for years. Instead of following their example and producing compatible trains and tracks, Cowen manufactured a train track in a different size gauge so trains manufactured by other companies would not fit on Lionel tracks.

This bit of folly could have ended his career in train manufacturing, but Cowen was confident enough to believe that his competitors would follow him. In 1908, the Lionel catalog made an outlandish claim by calling the Lionel line the "Standard of the World." As author Pierce Carlson explains, "But in a brilliant flash of inspiration, Cowen christened his non-standard, orphan gauge 'Standard gauge.' All other gauges by other manufacturers, from then on, would be 'non-standard' by definition—it was a breathtaking bit of gall but it worked." [19] Competitors eventually changed the size of their tracks to match Cowen's.

The Lionel catalog, introduced by Cowen in 1902, became an important advertising avenue. Lionel catalogs were printed and distributed to parents, children, and retailers. Nicknamed "wish books," they did not merely list the products they sold, but inspired dreams. Author Allan Miller explains their significance in the 1920s:

> During this period, the Lionel magic was displayed on the cover and inside pages of every new catalog, where beautifully drawn Lionel trains could be seen performing "real life" work against a variety of backgrounds representing different seasons, different railside environments, and different geographical locations. These catalog images inspired dreams of travel and adventure in many young minds, and when they eventually became older and more settled minds, the dreams were still there and capable of being realized, at least in part, because Lionel trains were still there, as well. [20]

Realities of War

When boys first started playing with Lionel trains, they imagined themselves to be train engineers or railroad tycoons. That focus shifted as American troops fought overseas in World War I. (Due to the anti-Semitism of this time, Cowen changed his name from Cohen to Cowen, a more neutral spelling.) Patriotism found its way into toy manufacturing. Cowen knew that toys had a great influence on children and how they thought. If toy trains made a boy want to be an engineer, a toy military train could inspire him to be a soldier or general. With that in mind, Lionel began producing an armored train set equipped to do battle. The 1917 catalog proclaimed, "Play War!" Train accessories now featured ammunition cars and military supply cars.

Lionel's advertisements showed boys happily pretending to be soldiers fighting an unseen enemy. At that time Cowen believed playing war was an innocent game all boys played. As the war in Germany raged on and newspapers reported daily on the atrocities of war, Cowen's attitude shifted. With Americans dying on the battlefield, war was no longer a game. Author Ron Hollander explains Cowen's change of heart: "By the thirties, he had developed serious doubts about the wisdom of urging boys to do something as contradictory as 'play war.'"[21]

When it was suggested that Lionel should manufacture a military gun on a railroad car and more realistic army accessories, Cowen refused and stated, "We are not desirous of bringing the idea of war to the minds of children. We would much prefer to devote our efforts and energy to the development of toys that are more elevating to the mind of a child."[22] Lionel was out of the war toy business for good, even if it meant the company would lose money.

Advertising Avalanche

By the 1920s, business owners were beginning to understand the enormous effect advertising had on consumers. Cowen bombarded the public with advertisements. Splashy and colorful ads for Lionel trains appeared in national newspapers. Radio advertisements were heard across the country. With the advent of television, Lionel commercials were aired. Aimed at children, advertisements appeared on the comics page in Sunday newspapers. Magazine ads appeared in *Boy's Life, Life, Look,* and *Popular Science.*

The advertisements would entice consumers into the store, and Lionel wanted the salesmen to be prepared. He published manuals describing how Lionel trains should be displayed in the store. Some layouts were built at Lionel and shipped directly to the retailers. Salesmen were given specific manuals on how to best promote and sell Lionel trains and accessories. The advertising campaigns were successful in increasing sales.

Mickey (Almost) Saves the Day

In the 1930s American railroads were in financial chaos. After serious trouble transporting needed war materials to the East Coast, the government took over and the USRA (United States Railroad Administration) was put in charge. Due to the Depression, people were no longer using passenger trains for pleasure trips or vacations. In-

Shoppers admire a toy train display in a department store in 1951. Toy trains—especially Lionel sets—were big sellers throughout the 1950s.

stead of replacing and updating old locomotives, they were sold for scrap metal. The poor state of the railroad industry was reflected in the dismal sales of toy trains.

Railroad travel made a significant comeback when the Union Pacific produced a sleek steam-powered passenger train in April 1934. The M-10000 boasted of its cruising speed—110 mph. After Cowen's visit to Union Pacific, Lionel began manufacturing its own miniature version of the M-10000, and the toy train industry received a much-needed boost.

Another boost for Lionel sales came from a most unexpected source—a cartoon mouse. That same year, Lionel teamed up with the Walt Disney Company. They produced the Mickey and Minnie Mouse Handcar. The two metal figures appeared to be pumping the handcar as the windup toy circled the track. It was cheap to produce and fun to watch. Between Mickey's huge popularity and the price of one dollar, it was an instant hit.

Another big seller was the Mickey Mouse Circus Train. It included a tin locomotive, three railroad cars, a Mickey Mouse engineer, and Disney characters traveling in the passenger cars. A cardboard backdrop with a drawing of a circus was included.

While sales of the more expensive M-10000 were steady and helped improve Lionel's financial standings, the media ignored it and latched onto the story that the Mickey Mouse handcar saved the struggling toy train company. Cowen knew good publicity when he saw it and did nothing to set them straight.

Woo—Woooooo

For years, toy train manufacturers tried different techniques to duplicate the lonely woo-woo of a train whistle. In 1935, Lionel engineers Charles Giaimo and Joseph Bonanno finally solved the whistle blowing problem. They used a miniature motorized fan that forced air up through resonating chambers and out a hole in the top. It worked on a similar system, and the chambers could be tuned like those in an organ.

Lionel's publicity department asked Bonanno if they could say Cowen himself had invented the whistle. Bonanno had no objections. The story that was repeated and embellished was that Joshua Lionel Cowen was strolling along one afternoon when he heard an unusual train whistle wailing in the distance. He sprinted back to Lionel's engineering department. Cowen led his men to the railroad tracks with an array of recording devices to capture the essence of that whistle, which would become part of Lionel trains.

It was a great story and the public loved it. It would have been an even greater story if it had been true. It was not the first time Cowen blurred the lines of reality and fiction or used exaggeration to make a point, nor would it be the last.

Lionel ads often used outlandish and exaggerated claims. Sometimes they even attacked the competition. One catalog ad proclaimed, "A FACT, If you want a miniature electric train to work satisfactorily as a toy or for Show Window Display YOU MUST GET A LIONEL." [23] Lionel angered many competitors with its inflammatory ads, but rules and guidelines for advertisements were not as restrictive as today. Nobody knows if Cowen used exaggeration as an advertising tool or if he really believed his own wildest claims.

Successful Advertising Campaigns

Cowen was always looking for new and different ways to promote Lionel trains. He did not believe trains were merely toys but rather an integral part of a boy's childhood. Lionel ads often featured a father and son enjoying the trains together while building a close bond with each other. Cowen built an advertising campaign around that special bond between fathers and sons. A 1950s ad declared, "Lionel trains make a boy feel like a man, and a man feel like a boy." [24] The father and son theme led Cowen to one of his wildest ideas, which became a reality on June 5, 1946, when he held a Father's Day party at the Lionel showrooms.

This was no ordinary party. To be admitted, men had to bring proof of their fatherhood. Over five hundred men showed up bearing birth certificates, hospital maternity bills, baby pictures, booties, and diapers. It was a huge success and helped drive home the idea that toy trains were an important element in a close father-son bond.

Cowen (left) explains the features of his latest model locomotive to a young train lover. People of all ages are fascinated by Lionel trains.

However, Cowen's joy with his successful party was short-lived. His wife, Cecelia, had suffered with a heart condition for years. After complaining of feeling ill on June 12, 1946, she died suddenly. They had been married forty-two years, and Cowen was devastated by the loss. He continued going to the office but was sad and inattentive. To cheer him up, an employee brought him a flower to wear on his lapel. Because it lifted his spirits, she continued to give him a flower for his desk every day after that.

Cowen began working long hours to combat his loneliness and to strengthen his company. As a result, Cowen was ready to launch another successful campaign by the Christmas season. He knew that many families set up elaborate holiday scenes under their Christmas trees. These displays included nativity scenes, ice skating ponds, frosted trees, snowmen, Victorian villages, and carolers. He pictured an oval track circling the tree. Soon, Lionel trains were sold as holiday displays and decorations. In just a few years, word spread that no Christmas tree was completely decorated without a Lionel train

A young girl enjoys playing with an electric train set. Lionel was the first toy train company to market to little girls as well as boys.

circling around it. By 1953, a Lionel Christmas train made an appearance in the White House when President Eisenhower had a train set up to circle the family's tree.

Lionel trains were so closely connected to Christmas that this was included in a tribute to him upon his death. Author Allan Miller explains, "When Joshua Lionel Cowen passed away in September 1965, *The New York Times* made it a point to observe that this man had made Lionel the third wing of Christmas, along with the evergreen tree and Santa Claus." [25]

Lady Lionel

Not all advertising tactics were as successful as the Christmas campaign. When Cowen wondered why trains should be marketed only to boys, his company set out to produce a train set targeted specifically toward young girls. The result was the Lady Lionel. It featured a pink locomotive pulling pink, blue, and buttercup yellow railroad cars followed by a blue caboose. It was a disaster. Lionel soon realized that the girls who played with trains wanted *real* Lionel trains, not a cutesy, patronizing version built just for them. The Lady Lionel quickly faded away, but Cowen learned an important lesson and began featuring mothers and daughters in the advertising promotions. It was the first time a toy train manufacturer targeted the whole family as a potential buyer.

Later Years

One evening in the late 1940s, Cowen was invited to play bridge with his niece and some other players, one of whom was Lillian Appel Herman. The two began dating and were married in 1948. They loved traveling together and often crisscrossed the country by train. Joshua, Lillian, and a group of Lionel executives even traveled to Rome to donate Lionel trains to the children of Italy. They presented the trains to Pope Pius XII. Lillian was humbled by the experience, but Cowen's curiosity was aroused. As author Ron Hollander explains, "Noting the beautiful straight lines of buttons down the Pope's white cassock, [Cowen] quipped as they left the audience, 'The only thing I'd like to know is, who is his tailor?'" [26]

Cowen was interested in photography and loved taking pictures on vacations. In 1954, he decided to capitalize on a 3-D photo fad. For less than half the price of his competitors, he sold a camera that took 3-D slides that could be seen in a special viewer. The camera was awkward to use, and only one person could view the slides at a time. The 3-D photo fad was short-lived, and the camera was discontinued a few years later.

A young boy is fascinated with the smoke rising from the stack of his toy locomotive. Lionel is famous for its meticulous attention to detail.

By the 1950s, Cowen had become a wealthy man. He loved to sit next to his chauffeur in the front seat and encourage him to drive his Rolls-Royce or Isotta Fraschini fast—even if it meant speeding tickets. His interest in cars took second place to trains, but Lionel did manufacture a racing automobile set in 1912. Sales were slow and it was withdrawn. Years later, in 1962, Lionel came out with another racing car set that was more successful.

As the Cowens grew older, they continued to travel by train and frequently vacationed in Hawaii. They had box seats for the opera in New York, and Joshua also enjoyed playing gin rummy, golfing, and fishing.

On September 8, 1965, Joshua Lionel Cowen died of a stroke in Palm Beach, Florida. He was buried in New York about a mile from where he listened to train whistles as a boy.

Lionel's Lasting Legacy

The toy train industry would not be what it is today without the contribution of Joshua Lionel Cowen. His toy trains were much more than simple toys and stood out among other playthings. As author Gary Cross explains, "Little could compare with the miniworld of the electric train set. It miniaturized a society of men with powerful machines. And it was all there at the fingertips of the boy at the transformer." [27]

Cowen's undying passion and fascination for trains sparked generations of train enthusiasts and hobbyists. To him a train represented the joy, wonder, and innocence of childhood. Trains were a way to bridge the generation gap between parents, children, and grandparents. His attention to detail in replicating trains modeled on actual locomotives, as well as the wide assortment of accessories and artistic catalogs, will always be associated with Lionel trains.

CHAPTER 3

Alfred Carlton Gilbert: Making Science Fun

Alfred Carlton Gilbert was born on February 15, 1884, in Salem, Oregon. He was the middle son of Frank and Charlotte Gilbert's three boys. Frank Gilbert was a successful banker, and Charlotte was a stay-at-home mom.

A Restless Child

As a child, A.C., as he liked to be called, tended the family's cows, gathered firewood, and trapped squirrels. A.C. still found time to spend with his friends. He was outgoing, and other boys looked up to him as their leader. Hauling wood was a difficult and dirty job, but A.C. managed to talk his friends into helping him lug firewood up a steep hill by building a wooden chute and rewarding them with a wild ride downhill.

A.C., a restless child, constantly developed schemes and executed pranks. For example, one boring night, he and a group of friends attempted to lift a burro up to the second floor of a college chapel with a series of belts. After a lot of tugging, pulling, and laughter, they realized the annoyed burro would not fit through the chapel window.

In 1892, the family moved to Moscow, Idaho, and A.C. was able to funnel his energy into a more appropriate direction. As he recalls, "It may not sound like it, but I did not spend most of my time raising the devil. Most of my spare time was devoted to sports—track, gym, wrestling, football." [28]

Moscow Athletic Club

By the time A.C. was twelve years old, he loved all athletics. He wrestled, played football, and practiced with a punching bag, chinning bar, and climbing ropes. A.C. turned his family's old barn into the Moscow Athletic Club and decorated the walls with circus posters. At fourteen, A.C. was organizing and running track meets. He took the backs off his father's broken watches and turned them into medals for the winners.

A.C. worked on the punching bag for hours, perfecting his boxing technique. When a traveling minstrel show went through town, he ran away to join them, calling himself "the Champion Boy Bag Puncher of the World." A.C.'s career was short-lived. His father caught up with him when he was less than twenty miles away and brought him home. But the idea of performing was firmly set in his mind.

"I Need a Volunteer from the Audience"

Besides athletics, A.C. loved magic. He practiced sleight-of-hand tricks, deftly slipping a coin between his fingers to keep them nimble. A.C. would sit in front of a mirror making coins, cards, and handkerchiefs disappear and reappear. His father was aware of his son's

Alfred Carlton Gilbert was an Olympic athlete and accomplished magician before becoming a toy maker.

fascination with magic, and when one of the country's greatest magicians held a show in the nearby Reed Opera House, he bought tickets.

At the show, Hermann the Great, draped in his black cape, had the audience mesmerized. Toward the end of his performance, he asked for a volunteer. Frank Gilbert had arranged for his son to be chosen, and A.C. enthusiastically assisted the magician in a series of tricks. The magician did not know he was about to be upstaged by his assistant, as the story is retold in the Salem Online History Project:

> At the end of the performance, the magician said to his young admirer, "Don't you wish you could do things like that?" Gilbert replied, "I can," and demonstrated tricks he had learned from a magic kit he had won selling the children's magazine *Youth Companion*.[29]

Hermann the Great was impressed by A.C.'s talent and invited him backstage. After teaching him a few more tricks, he encouraged A.C. to keep practicing. A.C. wanted to become the best magician he could.

As a teenager A.C. worked at a variety of jobs. One summer was spent on his uncle George's farm. Another was spent working as a flagman for the Northern Pacific Railroad. He earned extra money wrestling in impromptu matches in each town they stopped in.

Up, Up, and Over!

In 1900, the Gilbert family returned to Salem, Oregon, where A.C. attended Tualatin Academy. He excelled in athletics, setting a world record for pull-ups on the chinning bar and the running long jump. A.C. competed in gymnastics, wrestling, boxing, and football.

One of Gilbert's favorite sports was the pole vault. He could not afford an expensive spiked pole, so he improvised. He found a sturdy cedar post from a fence and sanded it down until it fit securely in his hand. He dug a small hole in the ground and planted his vaulting pole in the hole when he practiced sailing over the bar.

With practice, Gilbert qualified for the pole vault at the 1908 Olympics held in London. The day was fraught with controversy. Even though he had easily cleared the winning height, the British judges were concerned with his homemade vaulting pole and the small hole he had dug in the ground in which he had thrust his unique pole. Gilbert borrowed the spiked pole from his toughest competitor—the British pole vaulter—and once again soared over the bar. The judges awarded him first place, and he was presented with the winning gold medal by Queen Alexandria of Egypt. Soon other pole vaulters were using spikeless poles and placing them in a hole or box before they vaulted.

"Nothing Up My Sleeve"

Gilbert attended Pacific University in Forest Grove, Oregon, and later enrolled in Yale to pursue a medical degree. He loved the scientific side of medicine and the intricacy of surgery but felt he would become too involved with his patients. Gilbert did not want to face the emotional trauma of losing a patient. So, even though he graduated with a medical degree, he never practiced medicine.

A.C. needed money to help pay for his tuition fees and college expenses. He turned to what he loved most—magic. He called himself "Gilbert the Great" and began putting on magic shows. Professors and students were awed by his performance and wanted to learn to do tricks themselves. A.C. patiently tried to teach them the complicated sleight-of-hand tricks he had practiced for years. Realizing they wanted to do tricks quickly and easily—without spending time practicing—he created his first boxed set of magic tricks. Each set contained props and simple directions for performing tricks. He sold them for five dollars and continued working on harder tricks—often practicing with coins during class and meals.

Magic Business

After the Olympics, Gilbert married his fiancée, Mary Thompson, and a year later set up business with his friend and partner, John Petrie. The two loved magic and named their company the Mysto Manufacturing Company. They sold individual tricks and sets that contained simple tricks and props such as handkerchiefs, coins, and a decanter that magically changed one liquid into another. Most of their business was done through their mail-order catalog where the ads were hard to resist. As author Gary Cross explains, "They promised boys the 'secrets of the world's greatest magicians at toy prices.'" [30]

Gilbert also devised tricks and sold them to other magicians. His favorite trick was making a bouquet of roses appear out of an empty vase. Gilbert and his wife meticulously made the feather bouquets at home in their living room. Mary also helped with the bookkeeping and orders for the company.

Magicians were quite popular at the time. Harry Houdini with his illusions and daring escapes was constantly in the headlines. Because magic acts were performed all over the country, tricks and props were in demand everywhere. Gilbert's company was making a profit, and he frequently traveled on a train from New Haven to New York to demonstrate, promote, and sell his magic sets. Staring out the window on those boring train trips gave him the idea for his next project.

Building a Best-Seller

In 1911, Gilbert and the other passengers riding the train from Connecticut to New York City got a firsthand look at the electrification of the city. The construction of poles and power lines changed the landscape on a daily basis. Gilbert was fascinated by the workers using steel girders to hang the power lines. He recalls, "It seems the most natural thing in the world that I should think about how fascinated boys might be in building things out of girders." [31]

Gilbert wasted no time implementing his new idea for a building toy. That night he and Mary used the thin cardboard that came pack-

The steel girders in a building construction site like this gave Gilbert the idea for his Erector set.

aged with new shirts to cut out models of girders. After he had the pieces he wanted, he took them to a machinist who cut them out of thin sheets of metal. From his training as a magician, Gilbert knew the value of practicing and experimenting. He spent hours playing with the steel girders, wheels, axles, pulleys, pinions, gears, steel plates, nuts, and bolts designing structures and improving on the pieces. Using bolts to connect the girders made them capable of moving, which opened up numerous ideas for models. He added a lip on the edge of the girders so they could overlap and make longer girders. As he explains, "I put together hundreds of things—some of which worked and some of which didn't. I've often said that I have put together more bolts and nuts than any man alive or dead. And I had fun doing it, too." [32]

Gilbert was ready to start producing his Erector sets, but the Mysto Manufacturing factory was not large enough for the machinery needed to cut out sheet metal. He rented an old carriage factory nearby and worked long hours perfecting his new building toy. Because John Petrie was not interested in manufacturing Erector sets, Gilbert's father stepped in and bought out Petrie's share of the business. The company changed its name to the A.C. Gilbert Company. Petrie stayed on at the Mysto division, which still produced magic sets. Petrie devoted his time to their new sets, which included a whole magic show in a box, including a curtain, tickets, fake mustache, and a poster announcing the magic act. Gilbert focused on his new creation.

Spreading the News

In the early 1900s, half of all toys bought in America were manufactured and imported from Germany. Gilbert wanted to change that. He debuted his Erector set at the 1913 Toy Fair in New York, and it immediately stood out from other toys. As he recalls,

> The two things that made Erector stand out even at its first showing at the Toy Fair were its square girder, put together with only two bolts, and motion—things going around and up and down. Erector attracted attention and drew crowds. Some of the biggest buyers in the toy business gave me encouragement and advice and—more important—big orders. [33]

Erector also contained blueprints and instructions for building projects such as the Mysterious Walking Giant Robot. The construction kits were seen as appealing as well as challenging and were sold in toy stores and department and hardware stores.

The time was right for such an interactive and creative toy. The Wright Brothers were experimenting with flight. Alexander Graham

Bell and Thomas Edison had captured the nation's interest with their inventions. Americans were looking toward a future of technological progress. Gilbert brought the excitement of invention and creativity to children. As explained on the Eli Whitney Museum—Gilbert Project website, "Gilbert put into the hands of children the spirit of that era. Gilbert captured the hearts and minds of American children." [34]

Gilbert wanted to sell an entire concept of creativity and teamwork. He started a monthly magazine called *Erector Tips*, which featured photos of creations sent in by children. In 1915, an article titled "The Way of a Winner—The Life Story of a Famous Athlete" appeared. It was written by and about Gilbert himself. He wrote to children about the value of competition and hard work.

We Have a Winner

Gilbert believed competition was a healthy part of childhood, and in 1914 he came up with the idea for the first annual Erector set contest. He asked children to send him photographs of their creations—and received an overwhelming response of over sixty thousand. Gilbert decided to give away big prizes that children really wanted, whether they were practical or not. In 1915, first prize went to a young boy who built a working model of the Panama Canal. He received a real two-seater Trumbell sports car—even though he was too young to drive. Other prizes included a canoe, BB guns, bikes, hockey skates, and Erector sets. The following year, first prize was a Shetland pony.

Gilbert looked for other ways to promote his toys, including advertising aimed at parents. In 1915 he took out a full-page ad in *Good Housekeeping* magazine targeting mothers of wild, out-of-control boys. Gilbert explained that he understood boys and had an answer for the stressed out, frenzied mothers. An Erector set would educate, entertain, and keep boys safely occupied for hours—and out of trouble.

The majority of his ads were aimed directly at children. That technique contributed to his marketing success. As author Susan Adams explains, "He was, along with his other talents, a marketing genius. While most toy-sellers of the day aimed ads at parents, Gilbert aimed his at kids: 'Hello, boys! Make lots of toys!' said one." [35]

Additionally, Gilbert's ads spoke to children as if they were friends instead of customers. As he recalls, "It was not just good selling, as it turned out, but I meant it." [36] Many boys wrote back—one year he received over three hundred thousand letters from Erector fans.

Despite the high cost of his Erector sets, which were priced at five dollars and up when most toys cost less than one dollar, the company continued to thrive. Between 1913 and 1966, more than 30

The Wright Brothers flew this plane in 1903. The early twentieth century was a time of technological progress, and Gilbert designed Erector to give children the excitement of invention.

million Erector sets were sold, earning it the nickname "the world's greatest toy." The sets ranged from simple kits that built vegetable carts similar to those used by farmers to an elaborate top-of-the-line kit that weighed fifty pounds and could construct hundreds of models, including a five-foot-long airship.

Future Engineers

By 1916, Gilbert was thirty-two years old, and his company was one of the most successful toy companies in the world. He frequently stated his goal to help boys become successful men, and to help them on their way, he created the Gilbert Institute of Erector Engineering. Boys got a special brochure explaining the details of the institute. To obtain the rank of engineer, boys had to send in a photo of their Erector structure.

Gilbert's Institute of Erector Engineering inspired boys like this one to learn engineering principles by using Erector sets.

To become an expert engineer and then a master engineer, a budding inventor and builder had to have sold subscriptions to Gilbert's monthly magazine *Erector Tips*. Boys received printed diplomas and lapel pins. Those selling the most subscriptions got hired to demonstrate Erector sets in stores during the Christmas holiday.

Four-Minute Man

When World War I began in 1914, American citizens were asked to cut back on everything from gas to food. Men were needed to persuade the public to do their part for the war effort. A born showman, Gilbert was quickly recruited to become one of the Four-Minute Men. He made patriotic speeches during the four minutes between shows at the local movie theater. Gilbert spoke many times and occasionally joined other Four-Minute Men in singing uplifting patriotic songs onstage.

The A.C. Gilbert Company continued producing toys but also began making military equipment such as gas masks and machine-gun parts. America was rallying together and buying Liberty bonds instead of luxuries like toys. At that time Gilbert did not see a problem with encouraging the public to buy bonds instead of toys. He felt the war would be over soon.

Saving Christmas

In 1917, the war still dragged on. Americans were encouraged to cut back on all spending, even on Christmas toys. Gilbert did not feel children should have to sacrifice by being denied toys. As a boy he loved waking up on Christmas morning to packages spilling out from under the tree. He took out full-page magazine ads that proclaimed, "Don't Cheat Your Boy on Christmas Morning." Parents responded, and Erector sets showed up under the tree.

As the war raged on, the Christmas season of 1918 approached. The Council of National Defense met with different industries and businesses to determine what each one could do to help the war effort. Secretary of War Newton D. Baker believed all Americans must do their part to help win the war overseas—even children. Baker proposed a ban on all toy sales during the 1918 Christmas season.

Gilbert did not agree with the ban and headed to Washington, D.C., to confront Baker and his council. He and a group of toy makers marched to the navy building armed with suitcases full of toys.

Actor Douglas Fairbanks leads a rally for war bonds in 1918. Gilbert initially believed that Americans should support the war effort and buy bonds instead of toys.

The council thought it was a waste of time listening to toy makers plead their case that toys were essential for America's morale. Gilbert knew he had only a few minutes to get their attention—and change their minds. Gilbert stood up and spoke about what he knew best—boys and the importance of their toys:

> The greatest influence in the life of a boy is his toys. A boy wants fun, not education. Yet through the kinds of toys that American toy manufacturers are turning out, he gets both. The American boy is a genuine boy and he wants genuine toys. He wants guns that really shoot, and that is why we have given him air rifles from the time he was big enough to hold them. It is because of the toys they had in childhood that the American soldiers are the best marksmen on the battlefields of France. [37]

The council stopped yawning and listened as Gilbert spoke about the importance of toys in shaping a child's future. When he finished, the toy makers opened their suitcases and placed their toys on the table. Soon they were on the floor examining the toy submarines, tin soldiers, Erector sets, and puzzles. After playing with the assortment of interesting toys, the Council of National Defense decided *not* to ban toys that Christmas season.

Gilbert's contribution in getting the council to stop the ban probably would not have become well known if a reporter from the *Boston Globe* had not heard about the meeting and called Gilbert for an interview. Gilbert consented as long as the emphasis of the article would be on the council's reaction to the toys, not on him and his speech.

News spread, and the headline of the October 25 *Washington Post* was CABINET MEMBERS BECOME BOYS AGAIN. Gilbert was referred to as "the man who saved Christmas," and it stuck.

Making Science Fun

Even with the success of Erector sets, Gilbert grew restless. His wife, Mary, was used to this aspect of his personality. She recalled, "Why, he hasn't sat still five minutes since he was a baby." [38]

In 1917 he enlisted the help of a chemist and developed a children's chemistry set containing small amounts of safe chemicals, a scale, beakers, test tubes, an eye dropper, litmus paper, and a book of easy formulas and experiments. Next came a working microscope, which included a fly specimen on a slide. The flies were collected from the dairy barn housing the cows that kept company workers supplied with milk for their lunch breaks.

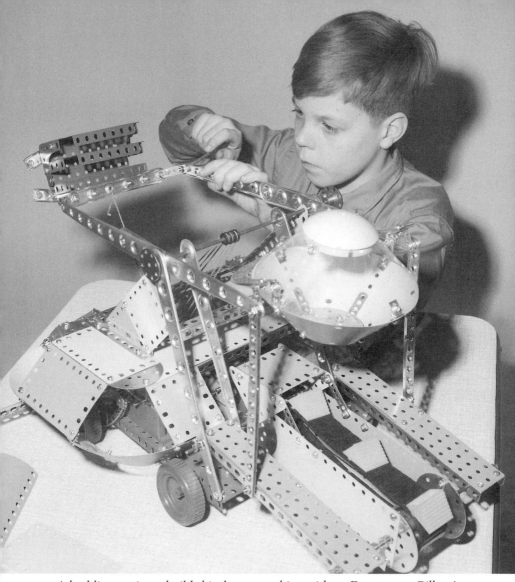

A budding engineer builds his dream machine with an Erector set. Gilbert's toys inspired an interest in science in children around the world.

The science kits were real, working minilabs, complete with manuals and instructions. Children could conduct experiments in the areas of physics, engineering, geology, light, sound, and magnetic fields. The Gilbert Hydraulic and Pneumatic Engineering Kit contained rubber tubes, stoppers, and spigots for curious plumbers. The manual contained 129 pages of experiments using water and air. An expanded line of science toys included weather kits, astronomy kits, amateur radio kits, and telescopes. Gilbert was one of the first to produce educational toys, and sales were promising. Fan mail from budding scientists reached two thousand letters a day in the early 1920s, attesting to their popularity. Gilbert opened a new manufacturing plant in Austria and several new sales offices across the country to keep up with the demand. (Gilbert was making over fifty thousand dollars a year—a fortune at that time.) Author Bruce Watson describes the effect of the science kits on a generation of children: "A.C. Gilbert made more than toys. He manufactured future engineers and scientists." [39]

Years later, those chemistry sets given as Christmas gifts had a strong influence on their owners as Yale professor Robert Treat Johnson discovered. Author James M. Schmidt explains, "After polling his students, Johnson identified chemistry sets as a factor in the great increase in the number of chemistry majors at Yale." [40]

Atomic Energy Lab

In 1950, Gilbert introduced one of his most ambitious and expensive science toys. The Gilbert Atomic Energy Lab cost fifty dollars, an amazing price for a toy. It was meant to educate as well as entertain. Gilbert had enlisted the aid of top nuclear scientists to help design the kit. It included a small amount of radioactive material and a working, accurate Geiger counter that measured radiation levels to ensure safe use of the lab.

Gilbert's goal was to teach children about atomic energy's usefulness in the world and to explain how it worked. Children, even with their parents' help, had difficulty understanding the scientific and technical manual. Children returned to their old chemistry sets and microscopes, and the kit was discontinued. Although not a success, it showed Gilbert's belief that children and science belonged together.

Last Years

Gilbert never stopped inventing. Besides his toys he created a fruit juice extractor, an upright vacuum cleaner, a heater, and a beverage mixer. In the 1950s, Gilbert spent less time working and more time enjoying the outdoors and hunting. While on Unimak Island in 1950, he shot a Kodiak bear, which he donated to Yale's Peabody Museum. After he retired in 1954, Gilbert traded his hunting rifle for a camera. He enjoyed making silent documentaries about Alaska's wilderness.

Throughout his retirement, Gilbert maintained his love of athletics, ran a mile every day, and practiced with a punching bag. Although he died on January 24, 1961, of a heart attack, his philosophy that play is education and science can be fun is still widely accepted decades later.

CHAPTER 4

Ole Kirk Christiansen: LEGO Brick Builder

Ole Kirk Christiansen was born in 1891, in the small village of Fil-skov, northwest of Billund, Denmark. Only eight tiny houses dotted the flat farmland. It was a desolate, lonely place visited once a week by stagecoach.

Bare Beginnings

The Christiansens were poor and everyone was expected to work to help the family survive. When Ole was only seven years old, he was given the important task of watching over their family's flock of sheep as they grazed on the nearby moors. Most children would have become lonely and bored during those long, quiet days. Ole Kirk spent his days scouring the ground and picking up sticks of wood. He studied the grain and texture of the wood and soon began whit-tling with his small pocketknife as he tended the sheep. Ole Kirk honed his craft as a woodcarver as he turned those piles of sticks into recognizable animal shapes.

His natural talent was soon apparent to those around him, and his parents felt he should explore the carpentry trade. Still a child, Ole Kirk was apprenticed to his older brother so he could expand his knowledge of wood and sharpen his woodworking skills. He spent his teenage years learning the basics of carpentry. Once he had learned all that his brother could teach him, he traveled to Germany and Nor-way to learn other woodworking techniques from master carpenters. Christiansen paid close attention to the other carpenters and con-stantly tried to improve his skills. As an apprentice he carried around a tattered notebook he called his "character book." He asked his em-ployers and coworkers to write down their comments on both his work habits and his personal habits in his notebook so he might im-prove himself. After completing his apprenticeship, he celebrated by buying himself a bicycle. Although Christiansen never had any formal classroom training, all the years of hands-on apprenticeship paid off as Ole Kirk struck out on his own.

Building a Business

In 1916, when Christiansen was twenty-five years old, he decided to settle down in his hometown of Billund. The town was once described by a traveler passing through as a "God-forsaken railway stopping point where nothing could possibly thrive." [41] Christiansen was intensely loyal to his family, friends, neighbors, and community. Although he could have found work as a carpenter elsewhere, he felt bound to the land of his childhood and decided to help improve the small village's way of life. Author Maynard Good Stoddard explains: "Ole devoted his life to not only proving that something could survive

Danish inventor Ole Kirk Christiansen created the wildly popular LEGO blocks in 1949.

Christiansen bought the Billund Woodworking and Carpentry Shop (pictured) in 1916. A fire caused by two of his sons later destroyed the shop.

in Billund, but that it could grow and prosper." [42] He bought the Billund Woodworking and Carpentry Shop and proudly became his own boss.

The bulk of Christiansen's new carpentry business was building houses, sheds, and barns during the summer months. The landscape of Billund changed as he placed the brick chimney on the new dairy he built—it was now the tallest structure in town. In the harsh winter months he built wardrobes, dressers, and chests of drawers. Although Christiansen kept busy, he was not making much of a profit. The local potato farmers were poor and could not always pay their bills. If they could only repay him with potatoes, he accepted the food gladly. After all, Christiansen and his wife, Kristine, had to feed their four young sons.

Christiansen believed his neighbors were an extension of his family and that it was his duty to help them in any way he could. That was demonstrated during World War I when he had signed a contract to build a local church. Building materials became scarce as the war dragged on and prices soared. Christiansen could not build the church with the amount of money they had agreed upon in the contract. Instead of abandoning the project or simply asking for more money, he built the church using his own funds—putting the financial future of his business in jeopardy. Afterward he commented that it was all done for a good cause.

Christiansen's nine siblings were aware of his remarkable carpentry skills and his poor sense of business. They encouraged him to abandon his business and look for more lucrative work. However, Christiansen was determined to keep his business going. Then in a flash, disaster struck.

FIRE!

In 1924, on a quiet Sunday afternoon, two of his sons, Karl Georg and Godtfred, were playing by themselves in their father's workshop. They lit a fire in the glue welter, and a spark caught a nearby pile of wood shavings on fire. The flames spread quickly, destroying the workshop and the adjoining house where the family lived. The entire family escaped without injury, but the woodworking business lay smoldering in ashes. Christiansen had worked too hard to give up on his carpentry business. He hired an architect to design a bigger, more impressive building to house his workshop. The family would live in a small, crowded apartment on the second floor. The rest of the building was reserved for his carpentry business. He also rented space to other local businessmen and craftsmen. No sooner was Christiansen open for business again when another tragedy occurred.

A Strong Faith

When Ole's wife, Kristine, died in 1932, he called upon his faith to help guide him through the grief-stricken days. Suddenly, Christiansen was left to raise four young sons alone. He spent time with them by teaching them about woodworking and carpentry, and soon they were able to help him out with his business.

Christiansen's faith, a crucial part of all aspects of his life, helped him deal with the trauma. Ole Kirk Christiansen's family were members of a Danish religious movement known as Indre Mission. His strong faith gave him an unshakable self-confidence and a feeling of optimism in all situations, no matter how dismal or traumatic. From the time he was a young boy, Christiansen felt a deep sense of duty— to his family, his neighbors, and his community. He never made a business or financial decision without first considering how it would affect those who depended on him. He did not feel burdened by his responsibility to his family and community but instead believed it gave his life purpose.

The Depression

In 1932, America was in the midst of an economic depression, which gradually had a negative effect in Europe. Businesses that relied on exporting their goods to America floundered. The hard times caused by the Depression trickled from the large cities to the small villages. In Billund, the farmers struggled and could not afford to build a new house or add on to an existing one. New furniture was considered a luxury.

Christiansen turned his attention to building only the most necessary household items, such as milking stools for the dairy farmers, stepladders, and ironing boards. He could not afford to waste such a precious commodity as wood, so Christiansen found uses for all the leftover scraps. He carefully carved miniature replicas of the products he was going to build to make sure they were economical and would fit together perfectly—with the least amount of waste. He used the tiny wood scraps to carve animals, buses, cars, airplanes, and baby carriages.

Christiansen was always striving to improve his craft, and that effort showed in his work. Instead of carving a simple fire truck, he created one that had a ladder that could be raised and lowered by a child. One coat of paint would easily chip, so he carefully applied several coats to each handmade toy. It was an unusual practice at that time because it took extra time and materials.

At first he gave the toys to his four young sons. Before long he had carved so many toys he went door-to-door and sold them to his neighbors. Even though money was scarce, Christiansen knew parents would want their children to have an occasional new toy.

Still Struggling

Times were hard for everyone in the tiny village, but Christiansen never lost his sense of optimism. He believed that the poor economy was temporary and good times were ahead. One buyer agreed and bought several of his unique toys, thinking they would be an inexpensive distraction for children and parents would happily buy them. Unfortunately the buyer went bankrupt, and Christiansen was left with a huge order for toys. Rather than let them sit in the workshop, he found himself once again taking his toys door-to-door to his neighbors. He traded the toys for goods, sacks of almonds, and whatever else they could come up with for payment.

Due to his generosity, Christiansen was again facing bankruptcy. His brothers and sisters dutifully loaned him money but told him he should stop wasting his time carving toys and work on something more useful. They did not realize Christiansen's love for making toys. He took the loan when it was offered and quietly returned to making toys.

Soon Christiansen had an inventory of over three hundred different wooden animals, vehicles, and dolls. One pull toy had a pudgy

Workers in Christiansen's shop paint wooden toys by hand. Employees submitted ideas for naming the company but Christiansen did not like any of their submissions.

clown grasping the handlebars of a green cart. His head bobbed up and down as the toy was pulled along behind a toddler. Christiansen's vision of the future was reflected in his line of sleek, brightly colored roadsters, airplanes, and trains.

And the Winner Is . . . Me!

By 1934, Christiansen was concentrating on toy making, and the business showed some signs of improvement—just as he had predicted. Sales picked up as word of mouth spread about his high-quality wooden toys. He felt it was time to officially name his wooden toy company. He held a contest among his small group of employees to find the perfect name. The prize for the winner was a bottle of his own homemade wine. Christiansen carefully sorted through all the entries but did not find one that was better than his own idea. So, he declared himself the contest winner and took his own bottle of wine back home. The prizewinning name was LEGO. It combined the Danish words

"Leg Godt," which means "play well." Years later it was discovered that LEGO is Latin for "assemble" or "I put together."

Crash of a Craze

In the 1930s the yo-yo fad swept across the United States and found its way to Denmark. Christiansen and his company wanted to share in its phenomenal success. He and a small group of employees worked day and night to produce high-quality wooden yo-yos, halting the production of other toys. Soon the warehouse shelves were crowded with boxes of yo-yos waiting to be shipped to toy stores and retailers.

Fads are unpredictable. Almost as quickly as the yo-yo craze hit, it began to die out. Once again Christiansen found himself with a workshop crammed full of finished toys—and no buyers. It would be a huge financial disaster that his company could not afford unless he could find a way to use the yo-yos and cut his losses. Christiansen

Ole Christiansen works on a model for a new toy. An extremely resourceful toy maker, Christiansen once used yo-yos as wheels for a new toy truck.

instructed his employees to carefully take the yo-yos apart, separating the two wooden halves. They looked like wooden wheels. Christiansen quickly designed a truck that fit the wheels, and production began again. The truck was an instant hit with children, and the yo-yos found a new home.

Just when one business crisis was averted, another one hit. In 1942, Christiansen's LEGO factory was destroyed by fire, but he quickly rebuilt it. The company now employed about forty workers, including all four of his sons, a fact Christiansen was proud of. He treated his employees like family members, and they became a close-knit, hardworking group. Christiansen even bought them a large area of land in Billund. After arranging the development of roads and a drainage system, he allowed his employees to build homes there. The major road was named Ole Kirks Vej in his honor.

Plastic Makes an Appearance

Christiansen had been carving simple wooden building blocks for years, but in the 1940s, a new material called plastic caught his eye. Christiansen firmly believed the new lightweight, durable material would revolutionize the manufacturing business. In 1947, he bought a plastic injection molding machine. It enabled him to melt plastic pieces and then inject them into a mold he had made in the shape of a toy. His first plastic creation was a baby's rattle shaped like a fish. By 1949, his designs were more complex. He developed a plastic tractor that could be taken apart and snapped back together, which gave the toy additional play value. He felt he owed it to children to give them toys that would help them use their imagination and involve them in active play. Christiansen kept improving the molds and felt the possibilities with plastic were only limited by the creativity of the toy maker. Not everyone agreed, however, that plastic was the best material for children's toys. One trade magazine at the time emphatically stated that plastic toys would never take the place of good old-fashioned wooden toys.

Building a Better Block

For generations children had stacked wooden blocks and built wobbly towers. Christiansen decided that improving upon the simple wooden block would show skeptical retailers the value of plastic toys. He developed bright, durable plastic blocks but was not satisfied that they were different enough from their wooden counterparts. After watching children stack blocks and easily knock them over, he decided the key to improving them was to make the blocks more versatile and to find a way to hook the blocks together—but not so tightly that a child could not pry them apart.

A worker polishes the body of a toy truck in Christiansen's factory. Christiansen always treated his employees like one big family.

After much trial and error, he came up with a basic design for an interlocking plastic brick. It had raised nubs on the top and hollow spaces on the bottom. It snapped together and could easily be pulled apart. Christiansen was pleased with his improvement on the traditional wooden blocks and believed they would open up a world of possibilities for budding builders. He called his new creation the "automatic binding brick." This new block eventually found its place in history, as author Wendy Woloson explains:

> Legos were certainly not the only building toys on the market during the better part of the twentieth century, but they were the ones that quintessentially represented the culture of the time. Wooden building blocks had been around for thousands of years and symbolized a simple, pre-industrial era.[43]

The employees of LEGO posed for this photo in front of the factory in Denmark in 1942. All four of Christiansen's sons were also employed at his factory.

When the automatic binding bricks were first introduced in 1949, they were sold only in Denmark. By 1955 LEGO bricks were exported to Sweden and then Germany. In 1958, the patent was granted for the unique locking design of LEGO bricks, and they soon became an international hit. Their success continued to soar, garnering award after award. Christiansen's LEGO bricks made a permanent name for themselves in the history of toy making by being named by *Fortune* magazine as one of their "Products of the Century" for having such an impact on U.S. history. Author Christine Chen explains:

> We were particularly impressed that after half a century, LEGO is still extremely popular with both children and adults. We also liked the fact that LEGO is truly a global brand, and that the colorful bricks appeal to both boys and girls who can play with them alone or with others. I remember spending many hours as a child building elaborate houses and spaceships. In fact, many of us here at *Fortune*

still have LEGOS in our homes. They're versatile, they stimulate creativity, and most of all, they're fun. [44]

Quality Is Number 1

The success of LEGO bricks could in part be attributed to Christiansen's firm belief that quality was the most important factor in producing merchandise—especially toys made for children. His motto was "Only the best is good enough." Christiansen's son Godtfred carved his father's slogan (DET-BEDSTE-ER-IKKE-FOR-GODT) on a wooden plaque in the 1940s and hung it in their workshop.

His passion for high-quality merchandise can be traced back to when he first carved wooden toys. Each one received three layers of paint—no more, no less. Later when his business expanded, he still

The LEGO brick has remained a popular toy for more than fifty years and was voted one of the "Products of the Century" by Fortune *magazine.*

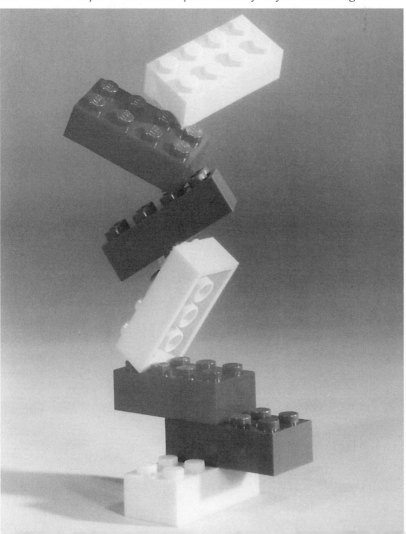

This photo of the LEGO factory in 1958 shows workers creating the famous LEGO bricks. Christiansen insisted on quality products, whether they were made of wood or of plastic.

refused to cut corners to save money and would not allow his employees to either. One of the LEGO company's most popular toys sold in the 1930s and 1940s was a colorful wooden duck pull toy. Godtfred Christiansen learned how important quality was to his father when he was in charge of a shipment of wooden ducks in the 1930s. He came up with an idea to help save the company money, thinking his father would be proud of him for taking the initiative. He decided to skip the second coat of paint on the wooden ducks. When he told his father what he had done, he was surprised by his negative reaction. Christiansen demanded that the entire shipment be called back and Godtfred had to repaint every single toy—no matter how long it took.

This insistence on quality continued when the LEGO company began producing plastic toys. Even now, all toys must pass a rigorous test before they are allowed to leave the factory. The toys are dropped, twisted, thrown, bitten, and checked for sharp edges. Only after they have passed the safety tests and quality checks are LEGO bricks ready to be shipped to retailers.

Christiansen succeeded in creating a unique and creative toy for children without compromising his high standard of quality. Mathias Tugores explains, "With his vivid imagination and carpenter's bench, [Christiansen] came up with an idea to make toys that will not only appeal to the natural creativity and curiosity of young children but are also durable." [45]

A Small Red Brick

Christiansen believed that his LEGO bricks were not a finished product when they left the factory and were shipped to stores. He felt it took a child's own imagination to truly turn them into a toy.

Christiansen believed that a child's own imagination transformed LEGO bricks into a finished product. Exhibitions like this one in Sweden demonstrated the fun of playing with the bricks.

To remind him of those core values on which he had built his business, he always kept one small red plastic LEGO brick in his pocket.

In 1957, LEGO celebrated its twenty-fifth anniversary in style. Christiansen, his second wife Sophie, and their daughter Ulla were present for the festivities. Christiansen's four sons posed on wooden horses for a newspaper photographer. Bouquets of flowers arrived from people around the world. A local band played for the jubilee celebration as Christiansen led the procession through the streets of Billund.

One year later, Christiansen died at the age of sixty-seven, after being in poor health for years. Family, friends, and employees grieved for the kind, humble carpenter.

Christiansen's motto, translated from the Dutch as "Only the best is good enough," hangs above these workers as a reminder of the importance of quality.

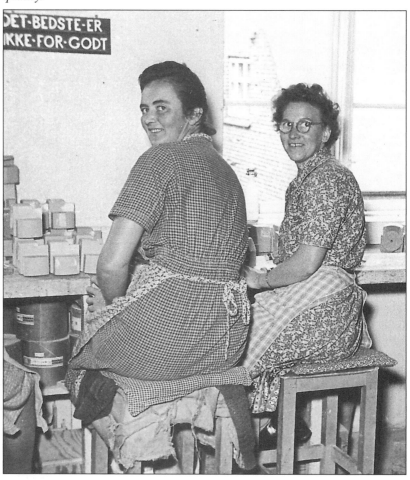

The combination of intellectual stimulation and good old-fashioned fun make LEGO bricks an enduringly popular toy. Its use is limited only by the imagination.

Years later, the LEGO company incorporated Christiansen's beliefs and ideals in a book of essays about children's educational development called *Serious Fun*. Combining intellectual stimulation and plain old-fashioned fun was what made LEGO bricks stand out from other toys. As Gary Cross explains, "This toy placed 'no limits on what you can build.' Legos promised to 'develop the child's critical judgment, manual dexterity, and ability to think for himself." [46]

Christiansen's Spirit Continues

Christiansen's goal was to create a toy that would inspire children of all ages to be creative. That ideal is still apparent in the many competitions and contests held by the LEGO company throughout the world. Each year the entries get more elaborate, complex, and unbelievable. Winning creations have included a robot that looks as if it is eating and digesting spaghetti, a working motorized lawn-watering device, and an interactive bird feeder. And around the world, an increasing number of LEGOLAND parks have opened. These theme parks feature life-size animals, buildings, whimsical characters, and replicas of famous monuments—all constructed from LEGO bricks.

The LEGO Bricks Builder's Legacy

Ole Kirk Christiansen wanted his toys to fully engage children, inspire their imagination, and teach them about the world around them. Christiansen realized his dream, and the LEGO brand has become internationally known, with sales in over 125 countries. Ole Kirk Christiansen was a quiet, hardworking man who had a true vision for creating an enduring toy, and he will be remembered for reaching and surpassing his goal—with great dignity and humility.

CHAPTER 5

Ruth Handler: Barbie and Mattel's Matriarch

Ruth Mosko was born in 1916 in Denver, Colorado. She was the youngest of Jacob and Ida Mosko's ten children. Jacob Moskowicz had immigrated to America from Poland in 1907. When he landed on Ellis Island, his name was shortened to Mosko. A blacksmith by trade, he boarded a train heading to Denver, Colorado, the center of the railroad industry at that time. In 1908, after a grueling trip across the Atlantic in the cramped steerage compartment, Ida Mosko settled in Denver with her husband and their six children.

A Strong Work Ethic

When Ruth was six months old, her mother had gallbladder surgery and was weak and frail. Ruth was taken in by her oldest sister, Sarah, and Sarah's new husband, Louie Greenwald, and remained in their home for nineteen years.

Although Ruth did not live in her parents' house, she inherited their strong work ethic and determination to succeed. Both of her parents had grown up in a poor Jewish ghetto in Poland. Everyone— men, women, and children—worked to help the family survive. Ruth felt she should contribute even though times were easier in America. She recalls helping Sarah and Louie in their drugstore:

> By the age of ten, I was working at the drugstore after school. Sarah and Louie didn't force me to work—I wanted to. And they paid me, though not much, because I felt I didn't need the money. I would walk to the store after school and wait on people, work the cash register, and be the soda jerk. I loved it. I simply preferred working over playing with other kids.[47]

Ahead of Her Time

In the early 1930s, girls were expected to grow up to become wives and mothers. Ruth had other plans. After graduating from East Denver High School in 1934, she was determined to go to college and

67

pursue a law degree. Although she received little encouragement from her family, she enrolled at Denver University.

During her summer break from college when she was nineteen, Ruth vacationed in Los Angeles, California. While there, she looked up an old friend who worked at Paramount Studios and offered to give Ruth a tour. When the two stopped for lunch amid the movie stars and film crews, Ruth asked how someone got a job there. Evelyn told her it was impossible. That answer struck a nerve. Ruth said, "Though I really hadn't been interested in pursuing such a job myself, that word *impossible*—even way back then—turned the idea into an irresistible challenge." [48]

Ruth Handler, the inventor of the Barbie doll, poses with one of her creations.

Evelyn showed her to the personnel office. Within an hour, Ruth had talked herself into a position in the stenographer's pool typing movie scripts. Law school was forgotten.

Ruth moved to Los Angeles and was followed by her boyfriend, art student Isadore Elliot Handler, who quickly found work designing lighting fixtures. The two married on June 26, 1938.

Ruth remained at Paramount Studios until 1941. During her time there, Ruth observed the department managers making what she felt were poor decisions. She and her coworkers frequently ran out of work and knitted at their desks to pass the time. Then suddenly, a manager would rush in with a pile of urgent assignments. This cost the studio many hours of overtime pay. Ruth thought she would be more diligent managing workers and delegating tasks if she ever ran a business. Those early lessons of setting priorities and being financially frugal would soon become valuable. The Handlers had dreams of owning their own business but had not decided what type of business to pursue.

The Making of Mattel

In the 1940s, plastic was an exciting innovation. Elliot and his partner, Harold "Matt" Matson, were fascinated with it. Elliot began making colorful bookends, bowls, and lamps to brighten up the Handlers' drab apartment. Ruth suggested he try selling some items. When asked what he should make first, Ruth suggested picture frames. Photographers were desperate for inexpensive frames during the war years. Ruth saw a need in the marketplace and felt the three of them could fill it.

By the fall of 1944, Ruth was a stay-at-home mom with a three-year-old daughter, Barbara, and six-month-old son, Ken. She loved caring for her children but was restless. She recalls, "One option was to wait until the children were grown before I returned to work, but that prospect filled me with dismay. What if by then, I'd lost my spark, my ambition, my powers of persuasion?" [49]

She decided to sell Matt and Elliot's plastic picture frames. With a suitcase full of samples, she marched into a large photography studio and left with a huge order. Then fate intervened. In 1943, while America was involved in World War II, President Roosevelt restricted all plastic for military use only. Bakelite, the most widely used plastic, was being used by the military for the first time to produce lightweight weapons and war equipment.

The Handlers would not be able to fill their first order for plastic picture frames. Undaunted, Ruth suggested using wood scraps instead. After some brainstorming and redesigning, Matt and Elliot gave it a try. The photography studio *doubled* their order. The three

Ruth and Elliot Handler hold two of Mattel's biggest-selling toys: Barbie and Ken dolls. Mattel was named for Elliot and his business partner Harold Matson.

celebrated by naming their new company after the two men: Matt and Elliot (Mattel). Later, Ruth reflected on that decision:

> It never even occurred to me that some part of "Ruth" by all rights, belonged in the name, since it was my idea to start with picture frames and I brought in that first big order. But that was 1944, and just as a woman got her identity through her husband in her personal life—you were Mrs. John Smith, not Sally Smith—should it not be so in business? [50]

Mattel's first employees were two sales representatives hired in 1944 to sell the dollhouse furniture to department stores. Those sales helped put the fledging company on sound financial footing.

Ruth loved the marketing side of the business. Determined to find an outlet for Elliot's designs, she set up appointments with major retailers. Many businessmen were surprised when they realized she was the spokeswoman for Mattel. Some even asked to speak to her husband before they would listen to her sales pitch. Ruth explains,

> In some ways, I got a big kick out of my unique situation. Certainly it was an ego trip to be the sole female in a room full of males, and it often gave me a strange advantage since they didn't quite know what to do with me. I confused them, so I often outsmarted them. And sometimes I was even able to teach them something. [51]

The doll furniture was selling well on the West Coast, but Ruth was not satisfied. She had heard about the prestigious Toy Building in New York City, where the best and brightest toy manufacturers in the world displayed their exciting new designs. Ruth did not know anyone in New York, but alone and armed with a suitcase full of samples, she boarded a train to New York City.

Ruth took her sample case to the Toy Building at 200 Fifth Avenue where toy retailers placed several orders for Mattel's dollhouse furniture. Its products would now be sold on both coasts—an important step forward in establishing Mattel as an up-and-coming toy company. In 1945, Mattel's first year of business, they made a $30,000 profit. But Ruth had her eye on the future.

In 1947, the Handlers found out how competitive the toy business could be. Elliot was proud of his work and talked about his new toy ideas with other designers. The Handlers soon discovered that another company had copied one of their new musical toys and was selling a cheaper and inferior toy based on their design. Unfortunately, it was a common though dishonest aspect of the business. Matt was devastated, since he had personally invested $10,000 in Mattel and was terrified of losing it. Ruth's sister, Sarah, and her husband, Louie Greenwald, bought Matt's share of the business and he retired.

Building a Toy Business

Elliot Handler was bursting with toy ideas. The Handlers took his love of tinkering with musical toys and combined it with popular radio and TV personality Arthur Godfrey's signature act—plucking his ukulele. No other toy company saw the potential in creating a toy musical instrument. Mattel came out with the Uke-a-Doodle. It was a blue- and coral-colored ukulele that made a twangy sound when strummed. It was the first of its kind and made the toy industry take notice of Mattel's innovative designs.

The Handlers gambled that more musical toys would be in demand. Elliot came up with a design for a toy piano with raised black keys. Instead of relying on conventional tuning wires, the sound was created by tapping on a sheet of stamped metal. Because it was the first toy piano that could actually be played by a child, it was considered by retailers and toy vendors to be the hit of the 1948 Toy Show. Mattel followed the piano with the Lullabye Crib, a musical Jack-in-the-Box, and several other music-making toys.

By 1951, Mattel had moved into a sixty-thousand-square-foot building with six hundred employees. Mattel was flourishing despite the fact that neither of the cofounders had a business background. Some of their decisions were viewed as strange by their business colleagues, and they were nicknamed the "odd couple" of the toy industry. The Handlers asked all their employees to call them by their first names, and their workforce was made up mostly of women of all races. Neither of these practices was commonplace in the business world. Because the Handlers believed in hiring whoever best fit the position, regardless of race, color, or gender, Mattel was honored by the Urban League for the company's hiring practices.

By 1954, Ruth and Elliot Handler had exhausted their ideas for musical toys, so Ruth studied popular trends of the day. At that time, television westerns like *Bonanza* and *Gunsmoke* were hits. Because little boys wanted to be cowboys, Mattel introduced the Burp Gun, named after the sound it made when fired. Other toy guns were on the market, but this was the first automatic cap gun that could fire fifty shots with one pull of the silver trigger. Then came the sleek replica of a Winchester rifle. Sales rocketed. The company was making money and still expanding. Ruth was ready for another big gamble.

M-I-C-K-E-Y S-E-L-L-S

In January of 1955, Handler made a decision that would change the toy business in America forever. A representative of ABC Television asked the Handlers to sponsor a fifteen-minute segment on a new children's program called *The Mickey Mouse Club*. Mattel would help pay the costs of producing the show, and in return they received airtime to advertise their toys. It was a risky move because Mattel would have to make a fifty-two-week commitment at the princely sum of $500,000.

Boys in the 1950s often dressed up as their favorite TV cowboys. Mattel identified this trend and began to manufacture toy revolvers and rifles.

If the company could not generate enough sales from the television advertising, Mattel would not regain its investment. If the show failed, the Handlers' money would be wasted. Handler called in her financial executive and asked, "If we spend the $500,000 for fifty-two weeks on television but the program doesn't produce the extra sales we need, will we be broke?" His answer was, "Not broke . . . but badly bent." [52]

Mattel's first commercial was crude by today's standards. A cartoon boy stalked an elephant with a Burp Gun. Kids loved it and four weeks later, over a million of the guns had been sold, leaving the Burp Gun warehouse empty.

After the first nationally aired toy commercial, the relationship between toy manufacturers, salespeople, and consumers shifted dramatically. Prior to Mattel's TV advertising, toys were purchased by adults on the recommendation of toy store salesmen. Eighty percent of all toy sales took place in the six weeks before Christmas. Now, for the first time, there was a direct link from the toy maker to the child, and toys would be marketed and sold throughout the year.

Gambling on the TV advertising campaign was not the only important decision Handler made in the 1950s. She was ready to launch an even bigger idea.

Dream Doll in 3-D

Handler had often watched her daughter, Barbara, and her friends play with paperdolls. Ruth said,

> Through their play, Barbara and her friends were imagining their lives as adults. They were using the dolls to reflect the adult world around them. They would sit and carry on conversations, making the dolls real people. I used to watch that over and over and think: If only we could take this play pattern and three-dimensionalize it, we would have something very special. [53]

Even though Ruth Handler cofounded Mattel, her ideas were not automatically approved. Decisions were made by a committee of designers, cost accountants, marketing managers, and financial executives. When she presented her idea for a three-dimensional fashion doll, it was rejected. In fact, her idea was rejected so many times she finally stopped talking about it. But she never forgot it.

In 1956, while the Handlers vacationed in Switzerland, they came upon a toy shop. Ruth and Barbara were both mesmerized by six eleven-inch-tall Lilli dolls wearing exquisitely designed ski outfits. Right in front of Ruth was the three-dimensional adult fashion doll she had envisioned for years.

She and Barbara bought several dolls. When they returned to the states, Handler showed the Lilli doll to Jack Ryan, the head of Mattel's research and design department. She had proof that a fashion doll could be produced. Handler gave Ryan her doll's specifications—right down to the eyeliner. When she was told American manufacturers would not be able to produce the doll at a reasonable cost, Handler asked Ryan to find a manufacturer in Japan. Jack Ryan succeeded.

The next step was to name the doll and design a line of fashionable accessories. Choosing a name was easy. "Barbie" was Handler's daughter's nickname. While the body was being produced overseas,

Handler focused on the doll's wardrobe. Dress designer Charlotte Johnson was hired. She immediately understood Handler's vision of Barbie's future.

The managers had been won over. Financial executives were cautiously optimistic in the face of Handler's unwavering conviction that Barbie would be an instant hit. The doll would not be slipped quietly onto toy shelves—she was going to be showcased at the biggest, most important toy show in the world.

Ruth Handler's daughter Barbara poses with a Barbie doll in Hollywood during a 2002 ceremony celebrating the doll's legacy.

Barbie's Big Debut

The 1959 Toy Show opened its doors on a warm March morning in New York City. This vast wonderland of new toys was spread out among two thousand showrooms. Toy makers vied for the attention of more than sixteen thousand buyers from stores all over the world. Handler was caught up in the excitement. Her creation, "Barbie, the

This 2003 version of Barbie styles her as the fabled longhaired Rapunzel. Barbie has undergone many transformations since her debut in 1959.

Teen-Age Fashion Model," was finally a reality. Handler thought Barbie would be the hit of the Toy Show.

She was wrong. Many buyers told her it would never sell, and at least half of them refused to place orders. One salesman took Handler aside and tried to explain Barbie's lack of acceptance. He said, "Little girls want baby dolls. They want to pretend to be mommies." [54]

Handler disagreed and was angered by the statement. After watching her own daughter, she knew that little girls dreamed of being bigger girls.

It soon became obvious that Handler was right. A few daring buyers agreed to stock Barbie, and the public's reaction was phenomenal. Mattel tripled the production rate from twenty thousand dolls per week to over sixty thousand, and it still took three years to catch up with the initial demand.

Handler's dream did not end with one adult fashion doll. Over the next few years, Barbie acquired a boyfriend. Ken was named after the Handlers' son. Then came Midge, Barbie's best friend, along with siblings, cousins, and pets.

By 1961, Barbie was testing the waters of various careers. She was a ballerina, nurse, and American Airlines stewardess. In 1973, Barbie became the first female doll in America with a medical degree.

Handler explains why she insisted Barbie be more than a clotheshorse. "At that time, before the advent of women's liberation, little girls believed that they would grow up to be either mothers or high-fashion models, and they generally were not encouraged to aspire to much else." [55] Not only did Handler truly believe that girls should dream big, she showed them the way through her own life.

Despite struggling against the prejudice against women in business, the 1960s were a successful time for Handler both professionally and personally. Then a health crisis brought everything crashing down.

Diagnosis: Cancer

In 1970, Handler discovered a cancerous lump in her left breast. Three days later she underwent a radical mastectomy—surgical removal of the breast, chest muscles, and lymph nodes.

Healing emotionally proved to be far more difficult than healing physically. Handler had lost her self-esteem and self-confidence. For the first time in her life, she felt she could not manage what was happening to her, and she slipped into a depression. Family members, friends, and colleagues avoided talking about the mastectomy. Support groups for cancer survivors would not be created for several more years. When Handler returned to work five weeks after her surgery, she discovered she had difficulty making decisions and

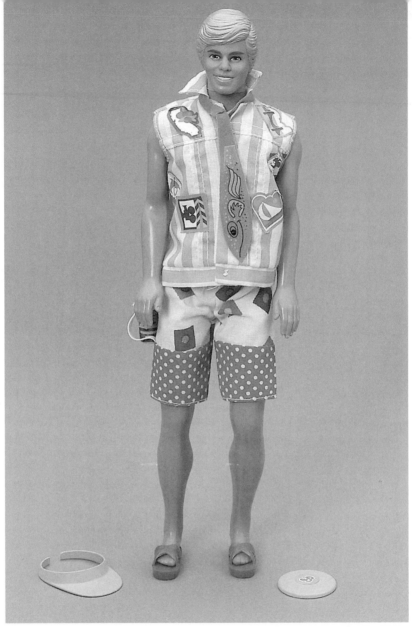

Barbie's boyfriend Ken, shown here as a surfer, celebrated his fortieth birthday in 2001.

delegating responsibilities—tasks she had never questioned before. As it became harder to focus her energy on Mattel, Handler felt the business side of her life was spinning out of control.

Career Crisis

Mattel began buying other companies so it would not be solely dependent on the toy market. It bought Metaframe, which produced pet supplies, and Turco, which manufactured playground equipment. Shifting the emphasis away from toys made the Handlers nervous, but they respected the business decisions made by their young, aggressive executives.

Mattel faced one crisis after another in the early 1970s. A plant in Mexico burned down. A shipping strike in the Far East cut off their toy supply. And internal problems were brewing closer to home. Mattel had grown so large that the Handlers could not continue to oversee all of the day-to-day operations. Discrepancies were discovered in the accounts. The Securities Exchange Commission (SEC) began an investigation into illegal business practices.

In November 1975, the SEC made the results of their investigation public. Mattel stood accused of making false earning statements. In 1978, a federal grand jury handed down an indictment for mail fraud, conspiracy, and making false statements to the SEC. The Handlers would be sent to prison if found guilty at a trial. Although they maintained their innocence, the Handlers agreed with their lawyers to plead no contest and avoid a trial. The Handlers each received a forty-one month suspended jail sentence, a $57,000 suspended fine,

A young Barbie fan grabs the newest model from the toy store shelf. Barbie is now an American cultural icon, and the doll is as popular as ever.

and twenty-five hundred hours of community service. In 1975, the Handlers left the company they had built from scratch.

New Direction

During Mattel's legal battles, Handler was fighting a personal battle of her own. Following her mastectomy she went shopping for a breast prosthesis and was discouraged at the only one available on the market. She remembers her disappointment: "I looked at this shapeless glob that lay in the bottom of my brassiere and thought, 'My God, the people in this business are men who don't have to wear these things.'"[56]

Handler had found a worthy cause and now had a new vision. She persuaded Peyton Massey, a brilliant prosthetic limb designer, to make a realistic breast prosthesis according to her specifications.

Handler rented a small factory, bought equipment, and set up production. This time, she would be a part of the company name. They called their new company Ruthton, a blend of Ruth and Peyton. Handler was back in business and doing things her way.

The Nearly Me breast prosthesis was a financial success, but more important to Handler, it fulfilled a crucial need for many women around the world. Through her company, Handler restored her self-esteem and helped other female breast cancer survivors restore theirs. In 1991, Handler began having heart trouble and decided to retire and spend more time with her family. She sold the Nearly Me corporation to a division of Kimberly Clark.

Remembering Ruth

Ruth Handler died Saturday, April 27, 2002, in Los Angeles. She was eighty-five years old. This petite, raspy-voiced dynamo fulfilled her dreams to succeed in the male-dominated business world and opened doors for generations of women to follow.

Handler had a unique, creative gift—summed up in a tribute to her in *Doll Reader:* "Many things have been said about Ruth Handler over the years, but the truest of statements is that she is a genius at spotting trends in our culture and then translating them into whatever project she is involved with."[57]

Ruth Handler will be remembered for her contributions to the toy industry, to cancer survivors, to little girls with career aspirations, and to anyone who has a dream—and the courage to make it come true. Barbie will go down in history as the best-selling doll of all time and the most recognized toy in the world. Author Kitturah B. Westenhouser makes an important point: "It makes us wonder now, is it the doll, Barbie, or her mother, Ruth Handler, who is really the legend."[58] Perhaps it is a bit of both.

CHAPTER 6

Lonnie G. Johnson: Super Soaker Inventor

Lonnie George Johnson was born on October 6, 1949, and grew up in Mobile, Alabama. He was the third of six children. His father worked at a local air force base as a civilian driver. His mother was a homemaker and occasionally worked as a nurse's aide. During the summer months, Lonnie and his two older brothers picked cotton on their grandfather's farm. In this environment, Lonnie's parents wanted him to learn the value of a strong work ethic.

Homemade Toys

The family sometimes faced hard economic times. Toys were an expensive luxury the family could not always afford. The Johnson children used their imaginations and whatever was close at hand to make their own toys. They turned bamboo tubes into weapons that shot unsuspecting enemies with chinaberries. An old lawn mower motor was used to power a homemade go-cart.

Lonnie was always tinkering, inventing, and experimenting when he was child. He frequently took things apart, figured out how they worked, and then put them back together. That curiosity for discovering how things worked continued throughout his life.

Blast Off!

Lonnie was a frequent visitor to the local library, researching any topic that happened to interest him at the time. One topic almost led to disaster. One day, as he was browsing through books in the library, he found the instructions and simple recipe for making rocket fuel. Lonnie could not resist brewing up his own batch at home. He mixed the ingredients together in a bowl in his kitchen and then heated up the mixture on the stove. The kitchen soon filled with black, billowing smoke, making it hard to see or breathe. Lonnie remembers that frightening incident: "The only thing I could do was back up." [59] The mixture exploded, and a kitchen chair caught on fire. Lonnie escaped without injury.

Unlike most parents, the Johnsons understood Lonnie's need to experiment and his insatiable scientific curiosity. They came to an agreement, as Lonnie explains: "My mother gave me a hot plate and told me to go mix the rocket fuel outside. My parents were very patient with me." [60]

The exploding batch of rocket fuel was not the only time he courted disaster when he was experimenting. When he was thirteen years old, he built a missile out of an old television antenna. It blew up before it left the launching pad. A year later Lonnie was questioned by the local police after rocket fuel ignited a small fire in the hallway of his high school.

Despite these setbacks, Lonnie kept tinkering and experimenting, learning from his mistakes and failures. His love of science earned him the nickname "Professor" among his friends, classmates, and neighbors while he was in school.

Linex

As a child, Lonnie loved watching the science fiction television show *Lost in Space* about the Robinson family traveling around the solar system looking for a way back to Earth. His favorite character was the robot. Lonnie was fascinated with robots and researched them at the library. He began scavenging through junkyards looking for odd bits and pieces to build his own robot. He dismantled his brother's walkie-talkies for the parts. His sister's reel-to-reel tape recorder became the robot's eyes. His love of robotics and years of picking through junk resulted in a three-foot-tall, remote-controlled robot named Linex, which ran on compressed air. In 1968, as a high-school senior, Lonnie won first place at the University of Alabama Junior Engineering Technical Society Exposition with Linex. He explains how unique his entry in the competition was at that time: "Back then, robots were unheard of, so I was one of only a few kids in the country who had his own robot." [61]

Almost at the same time he was celebrating his science victory, he received some disappointing news. Lonnie had taken a test given by the school's science club. When the results were tabulated, he was told he had "little aptitude for engineering" [62] and was encouraged to pursue other nonscientific career paths. He chose to ignore that advice; he wanted to become a nuclear scientist.

A Determined Scholar

Despite Johnson's lack of support and encouragement from teachers and school counselors, he was determined to go to college. His aptitude for math and fantastic SAT scores won him a math scholarship to Tuskegee University.

Lonnie Johnson poses with his first invention, Linex the robot. Linex won Johnson first prize at a college engineering exposition in 1968.

While in college he set a goal to work in the nuclear power industry after graduation. To prepare himself, he studied atomic fission in college. He proved the naysayers wrong when he graduated with distinction in 1972 with a bachelor of science degree in mechanical engineering. Two years later he received his master's degree in nuclear engineering. He not only excelled in college but was elected to the Pi Tau Sigma National Engineering Honor Society.

After graduation, Johnson was called to active duty as a second lieutenant in the United States Air Force. Assigned to the air force weapons laboratory in Albuquerque, New Mexico, he performed safety reviews for U.S. space missions such as *Voyager* that used nuclear power sources.

In 1979, Johnson went to work at the Jet Propulsion Laboratory in Pasadena, California, as a systems engineer. He was part of a

The Jupiter space probe Galileo *(pictured) was fitted with a revolutionary atomic power plant invented by Lonnie Johnson in the 1980s.*

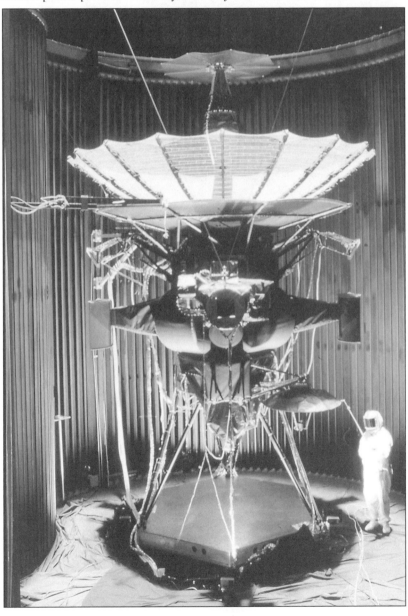

team working on the $1.6 billion Jupiter space probe *Galileo*. One aspect of the project was to incorporate an atomic power plant onto the spacecraft. During the course of the project, the engineers encountered a major problem. Although the spacecraft was designed to recover from major hardware failures that could occur during the mission, a power loss could destroy the computer memory. Its complete memory was necessary for the Jupiter exploration mission. Rather than accept a marginal solution, Johnson proposed a radically different approach. Despite skepticism from some of the best engineers and scientists in the country, Johnson's power system was successfully implemented. Years later, the system is still operating, and *Galileo* is sending data back to scientists on Earth.

That was not the only time Johnson's creative thinking was noticed. As *Gailieo* project supervisor Matt Landano explains, "Lonnie found extremely innovative solutions for problems—he always had a fresh approach and came up with ideas no one had thought of before." [63]

Super Squirt

In 1982, Johnson decided to experiment with refrigeration at home after work. It was standard procedure for refrigerators to use freon as a cooling device. Freon is a gas that can destroy the ozone layer protecting Earth from the harmful ultraviolet rays of the sun. Looking for a safer coolant, Johnson experimented with water. It was safe for the environment, inexpensive, readily available, and efficient.

He was tinkering at home when he hooked up a nozzle and hose to the faucet in his bathroom sink. There was air in the hose, and a large surge of air pressure forced the water to shoot out. Turning, he blasted a stream of water across the room, sending the shower curtain swirling from the force. He immediately saw the potential for an amazing water gun using air pressure as a propellant.

Johnson knew he could make a self-contained gun, complete with an air-holding tank, that could easily be pumped by a child. He built a model of his ideal water gun out of things he found around the house: a trigger pumped air into a piece of PVC pipe, and an empty plastic Coke bottle held the water. With a small machine shop already set up in his home, he had everything he needed to make the gun's pump parts, valves, and seals. The first prototype cost about ten dollars to make. His design relied on air pressure and arm pumping for pressurizing the firing chamber. Johnson let his six-year-old daughter, Aneka, take it for a test run. She tried it out on children in the neighborhood, and it was an immediate success.

Vive la Différence

Squirt guns had been around for a long time, but Johnson knew he had come up with something new and unique. Previous water guns worked on a simple system. As the trigger is squeezed, water is forced into a small chamber, through a narrow opening, and out toward its target. The guns held a small amount of water, and the tiny stream did not carry over a distance of more than a few feet.

Johnson did not use a traditional small water pump in his design. He realized that if the gun was pumped repeatedly, a large amount of energy could be stored as compressed air to push the water out with a much stronger force. The pumped air flowed into a chamber filled with water. The pressure built until the trigger was pulled, and the water blasted out up to fifty feet.

Safety was an immediate concern for Johnson. His water gun had a built-in relief valve that limited how high the pressure could go, to prevent the stream of water from becoming painful. Also, the stream of water was wide and dispersed rather than narrow and concentrated.

It was important for Johnson to protect his invention with a patent. As he explains,

> Back then I could not afford to pay an attorney to write my own patents so I went to the library and began researching it myself. I filed and prosecuted my own patent application. The whole process turned out to be a tremendous learning experience which helped me immensely both from an educational and financial standpoint.[64]

On October 14, 1983, Johnson officially applied for a patent for his first water gun. U.S. Patent No. 4,591,071 was granted for "a squirt gun which shoots a continuous high-velocity stream of water. The squirt gun [allows] . . . partial filling with water leaving a void for compressed air."[65]

Selling the Soaker

Johnson believed his high-powered water gun would be a hit if he could get it produced and sold to the public. Initially he wanted to make and sell the Super Soaker himself, and he returned to the library for help. He researched the manufacturing process and discovered it would cost him $200,000 to make the first one thousand water guns, a hefty $200 per gun. Because Johnson could not afford to manufacture them himself, he wrote to over twenty toy companies telling them about his invention and why it would be an asset to their company. Unfortunately, the response was dismal.

Setbacks and Roadblocks

Only one toy company responded to his letter about manufacturing his Super Soaker. Before any arrangements could be made, the company went out of business. Johnson kept writing letters and contacting toy companies.

Johnson poses with a copy of the patent he obtained for the Super Soaker. Unable to afford a lawyer, Johnson filed the patent application himself.

The next company to show an interest in his invention was the Daisy Company, manufacturers of compressed air BB guns. From 1985 to 1987, Johnson worked closely with the company to fine-tune his water gun (to make it easier for a child to operate) and to start the long process of getting it mass-produced. At that time, Daisy was undergoing several changes. A rapid turnover of key personnel meant Johnson had to start over each time a new manager took over the new products division. Each manager had unique ideas about manufacturing and marketing the Super Soaker. Ultimately, the licensing contract between Johnson and Daisy was not fulfilled. Johnson found himself right back at the beginning—searching for a toy company to produce his water gun.

Trying Again

In 1987, Intertech, a subsidiary company of MCA Records, entered the picture. Johnson had been working on other toys, and he first approached them with two other ideas. One was a vibrating toy machine gun and the other a toy airplane propelled by water. Using water as a propellant made the toys much safer and easier for childred to use than traditional toys propelled by burning hydrogen and oxygen. During the meeting with Intertech executives, Johnson mentioned that he had also developed a sophisticated water gun that could easily outperform and out-blast the ones Intertech was currently producing. It was a bold statement to make, but the executives were intrigued. They agreed to offer him a contract for the toy machine gun and the water-propelled airplane, but only after they saw the water gun he had bragged about. Johnson set about constructing a new model of his water gun. Two weeks later he handed the Intertech executives a Super Soaker. They were amazed at how superior it was to any existing water gun on the market—even the battery powered water guns they produced and sold.

Johnson's hopes and dreams of seeing his water gun sold to the public were dashed again. Intertech manufactured about sixty thousand of Johnson's airplanes but then began having financial trouble and went out of business in 1989. They never produced his water gun. While Johnson began the search for yet another toy company, he spent time tweaking and improving his water gun. All previously manufactured plastic squirt guns had one design flaw in common. The reservoir holding the water was made from two plastic halves glued together. That proved unreliable with a water gun using pressure. Johnson created a water reservoir from molding one single piece of plastic. Now there were no seams to leak or break. It was the key improvement that would make his water guns inexpensive and durable for mass production.

Right Place, Right Time

After eight frustrating years of trying to find a toy company to manufacture his water gun, Johnson found himself at the Toy Fair in New York City. Cautiously he approached the Larami Corporation with his water gun idea. As Al Davis, executive vice president of the company recalls, "He was dejected. He told me he had this amazing water gun that nobody would manufacture." [66]

Johnson was invited to stop by the Larami Corporation if he was ever in Philadelphia. Two weeks later in March of 1989, he showed up in Philadelphia with a battered pink suitcase containing a newly built prototype. He also had with him the paperwork required to protect the rights to his invention. Johnson was invited into the boardroom to demonstrate his water gun. He got the executives' attention when he aimed, fired, and blew their coffee cups right off the conference table. Larami's president, Myung Song, looked on in surprise and uttered, "Wow!" [67]

Although excited by their enthusiasm, Johnson was not ready to start celebrating. His previous deals had fallen through before production started. At Larami things were different. A few months later, company executives were showing prototypes of the Super Soaker to buyers. Production began on schedule, and it hit the stores the following January.

Celebrity Soaker

When Super Soakers first hit the stores, sales were rapid, mostly by word of mouth. The water gun got a huge boost when it was featured on a popular late night television show. In December of 1990, Johnny Carson, host of *The Tonight Show,* featured new and interesting products, just in time for holiday shopping. Larami had sent a Super Soaker to the show, and it was going to be one of the toys demonstrated and reviewed. Carson tried the other toys first. He was not impressed when several broke or failed to live up to expectations. Then it was time to test the Super Soaker on national television.

Carson fired the water gun and sprayed the audience. The reaction was immediate—the Super Soaker was a hit! The audience was amazed and delighted when Carson turned the water gun on his co-host and sidekick, Ed McMahon, and fired a direct hit.

The endorsement on *The Tonight Show* helped boost sales almost overnight. Advertising went nationwide in 1991 when the *Super Soaker* was featured in commercials. Sales continued to soar, and over 10 million water guns were sold within the first two years of production. Bigger and better models kept coming out, such as the Speed

Johnson poses with his most famous invention, the Super Soaker. Johnson spent eight years trying to find a manufacturer for his water gun.

Loader, Super Soaker Blaster, Splashzooka, and CPS-3000, which comes complete with a two-gallon backpack for easy reloading.

Branching Out

While trying to garner attention with his water gun, Johnson continued inventing other toys such as a car that is launched from a pad by air pressure. When the car zooms off the pad, a sound generator makes realistic motor rumblings. He also came up with an airplane powered by rubber bands—with a specially designed feature for quick winding and launching. With safety in mind, Johnson created a rocket with a safe rubber band launching system. After blasting off, the rocket gently glides back to the ground with its own parachute. The list is varied and intriguing. He came up with the idea for hair rollers that dried the hair as it curled. He created a digital thermostat and a home radon detector. Johnson also created a device that tests and measures the amount of moisture in soil and automatically activates the lawn sprinkling system when watering is required. One of his most ingenious inventions was a baby diaper monitor. When the diaper becomes wet, a musical nursery rhyme plays to alert the caregiver that it's time for a change.

Moving On

Johnson had many more ideas in his head that he wanted to work on. With the success of Super Soaker, he had the financial means to make those dreams a reality. In 1991, he used the royalties from sales of his Super Soaker to fund his own research laboratory, Johnson Research & Development, in Smyrna, Georgia, a suburb of Atlanta. The company focuses on several different projects including environmental friendly products.

Even after the establishment of his research laboratory, Johnson is still involved in the Super Soaker product line. He has also been active in another popular toy line—Nerf—using compressed air system. As Johnson comments, "Most of the new Nerf guns are our inventions." [68] He adds, "We're doing for Nerf guns what we did for water guns. They shoot farther, better, faster." [69]

Johnson will talk about Nerf in general terms, but when asked for details about his upcoming Nerf weapons during an interview with writer Michael Klein, he became cautious and mysterious, saying simply, "You can't write about that." [70]

It seems a strange combination to work on complex scientific designs and toy weapons, but one makes the other possible. As author Christy Oglesby explains, "Johnson said it was difficult to get financial support to develop more serious inventions. The sale of his popular toys such as the Super Soaker and the Nerf Wildfire dart gun have financed his other experiments." [71]

Johnson's research company concentrates on the needs of scientists and tinkerers like himself. Since he always felt he got his best ideas when working on a different project or while daydreaming, he insists on a relaxed and casual atmosphere for his employees so as to encourage creative thinking. They have flexible hours because Johnson does not believe creativity should be relegated to certain hours of the day. Employees wear comfortable shorts and T-shirts to work every day.

Johnson's goals for his company are "to push the boundaries of technology, to break new ground, and to refine technology so that it is accessible to the masses." [72] He has never forgotten how many years it took him to get his Super Soaker produced or the seemingly endless obstacles in the way. He hopes to alleviate some of those problems for future inventors. One division of his company is devoted to helping new inventors with sound advice on every aspect from properly filling out patent applications to finding funding for their projects.

Spreading the Message

Lonnie Johnson enjoys talking to groups of children about his inventions. He explains propulsion to the group and shares stories about his job experiences working on three different space probes for NASA. Johnson talks about the excitement of scientific challenges—both big and small—and the importance of education in children's lives. He pauses in his talk to squirt the attentive audience with a Super Soaker.

Although he holds over eighty patents in his name, with many more in the early stages, Johnson is most closely associated with the

Johnson works on one of his inventions at his research facility in Georgia. His company develops many types of useful products in addition to toys.

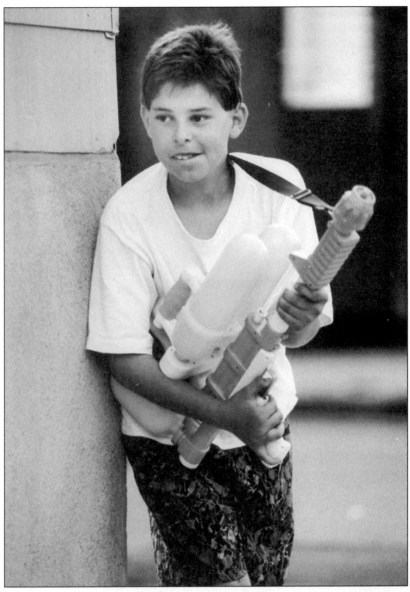

A boy enjoys playing with a Super Soaker. Lonnie Johnson's designs have made many toys safer and easier to use.

Super Soaker. He is pleased that children already know about it, which gives him a conversation starter. He is proud of what he has achieved and wants to share his success with children. As he explains,

> In a sense, it's my responsibility that they know [an African American is responsible for the creation]. If there are kids

who need strong role models and who need confidence and to be able to believe in themselves, then I want to be able to do that.[73]

Having a strong and deep belief in himself is what keeps Johnson striving to succeed. He shares the story of his struggle with others and offers encouragement and advice to all would-be inventors:

Persevere. That's what I always say to people. There's no easy route. Nobody's going to step in and dump a lot of money and make it easy. Unless you have a lot of money, you have to pay your dues and make a personal sacrifice.[74]

Lonnie Johnson's perseverance paid off. Super Soaker is a best-selling toy, and its use of compressed air has been adapted for other toys, making them safer and easier for children to operate. Not only has he made contributions to the toy industry and the scientific community, but his company encourages inventors to follow their dreams—just as he has.

Notes

Introduction: A Tale of Toy Makers

1. Elliot Handler, *The Impossible Is Really Possible.* New York: Newcomen Society of North America, 1968, p. 7.

2. Quoted in Harry L. Rinker, *Collector's Guide to Toys, Games, and Puzzles.* Radnor, PA: Wallace-Homestead, 1991, p. 5.

Chapter 1: Milton Bradley: Game Master

3. Milton Bradley Company, *Milton Bradley: A Successful Man.* Springfield, MA: Milton Bradley, 1910, p. 5.

4. Quoted in James J. Shea, *It's All in the Game.* New York: G.P. Putnam's Sons, 1960, p. 35.

5. Quoted in Bruce Whitehill, *Games: American Boxed Games and Their Makers, 1822–1992.* Radnor, PA: Wallace-Homestead, 1992, p. 11.

6. G. Wayne Miller, *Toy Wars: The Epic Struggle Between G.I. Joe, Barbie, and the Companies That Make Them.* New York: Times Books, 1998, p. 40.

7. Quoted in Roy P. Basler, *Abraham Lincoln: His Speeches and Writings.* New York: World, 1946, p. 562.

8. Quoted in Whitehill, *Games,* p. 11.

9. Quoted in Whitehill, *Games,* p. 11.

10. Shea, *It's All in the Game,* p. 80.

11. Quoted in Shea, *It's All in the Game,* p. 110.

12. Quoted in *Milton Bradley,* p. 44.

Chapter 2: Joshua Lionel Cowen: A Passion for Trains

13. Quoted in Ron Hollander, *All Aboard! The Story of Joshua Lionel Cowen and His Lionel Train Company.* New York: Workman, 2000, p. 22.

14. Joseph J. Fucini and Suzy Fucini, *Entrepreneurs: The Men and Women Behind Famous Brand Names and How They Made It.* Boston: G.K. Hall, 1985, p. 3.

15. Marvin Kaye, *The Story of Monopoly, Silly Putty, Bingo, Twister, Frisbee, Scrabble, Et Cetera.* New York: Stein and Day, 1973, p. 29.

16. Allan W. Miller, *Getting Started with Lionel Trains*. Iola, WI: Krause, 2001, p. 13.

17. Hollander, *All Aboard!* p. 27.

18. Fucini, *Entrepreneurs*, p. 4.

19. Pierce Carlson, *Toy Trains: A History*. New York: Harper & Row, 1986, p. 85.

20. Quoted in Miller, *Getting Started with Lionel Trains*, p. 16.

21. Quoted in Hollander, *All Aboard!* p. 63.

22. Quoted in Hollander, *All Aboard!* p. 63.

23. Peter H. Riddle, *America's Standard Gauge Electric Trains: Their History and Operation, Including a Collector's Guide to Current Values*. Norfolk, VA: Antique Trader Books, 1998, p. 14.

24. Fucini, *Entrepreneurs*, p. 4.

25. Quoted in Miller, *Getting Started with Lionel Trains*, p. 16.

26. Quoted in Hollander, *All Aboard!* p. 219.

27. Quoted in Gary Cross, *Kids' Stuff: Toys and the Changing World of American Childhood*. Cambridge: Harvard University Press, 1997, p. 54.

Chapter 3: Alfred Carlton Gilbert: Making Science Fun

28. A.C. Gilbert with Marshall McClintock, *The Man Who Lives in Paradise*. New York: Rinehart & Company, 1954, p. 55.

29. Quoted in Salem Oregon Online History Project, "A.C. Gilbert," December 2002. http://salemhistory.net.

30. Quoted in Cross, *Kids' Stuff*, p. 61.

31. Gilbert, *The Man Who Lives in Paradise*, p. 119.

32. Quoted in Bruce Watson, *The Man Who Changed How Boys and Toys Were Made*. New York: Viking, 2002, p. 18.

33. Gilbert, *The Man Who Lives in Paradise*, p. 128.

34. Quoted in Eli Whitney Museum, "A.C. Gilbert." www.eli whitney.org.

35. Quoted in Susan Adams, "Boy Toy," *Forbes*, November 11, 2002, p. 198.

36. Gilbert, *The Man Who Lives in Paradise*, p. 130.

37. Quoted in Watson, *The Man Who Changed How Boys and Toys Were Made*, p. 99.

38. Quoted in Watson, *The Man Who Changed How Boys and Toys Were Made,* p. 75.

39. Quoted in Watson, *The Man Who Changed How Boys and Toys Were Made,* p. 4.

40. Quoted in James M. Schmidt, "Yesterday's Toy Becomes Tomorrow's Trade," *Today's Chemist at Work,* September 2000.

Chapter 4: Ole Kirk Christiansen: LEGO Brick Builder

41. Quoted in Maynard Good Stoddard, "The Toy That Built a Town," *Saturday Evening Post,* October 1984.

42. Quoted in Stoddard, "The Toy That Built a Town."

43. Quoted in Wendy Woloson, "Legos," St. James Encyclopedia of Pop Culture. www.findarticles.com.

44. Quoted in Christine Chen, "LEGO Toys Named 'Product of the Century,'" *Business Wire,* December 2, 1999. www.business wire.com.

45. Quoted in Mathias Tugores, "Legoland," *Sojourn Online,* December 1999. www.sojournonline.com.

46. Quoted in Cross, *Kids' Stuff,* p. 169.

Chapter 5: Ruth Handler: Barbie and Mattel's Matriarch

47. Ruth Handler with Jacqueline Shannon, *Dream Doll: The Ruth Handler Story.* Stamford, CT: Longmeadow Press, 1994, p. 17.

48. Handler, *Dream Doll,* p. 28.

49. Quoted in Alan Farnham, *Forbes Great Success Stories.* New York: John Wiley & Sons, 2000, p. 71.

50. Handler, *Dream Doll,* p. 60.

51. Handler, *Dream Doll,* p. 112.

52. Handler, *Dream Doll,* p. 83.

53. Quoted in M.G. Lord, *Forever Barbie: The Unauthorized Biography of a Real Doll.* New York: William Morrow, 1994, p. 30.

54. Quoted in Miller, *Toy Wars,* p. 69.

55. Quoted in Billy Boy, *Barbie: Her Life and Times and the New Theater of Fashion.* New York: Crown, 1987, p. 22.

56. Quoted in Farnham, *Forbes Great Success Stories,* p. 81.

57. Glenn A. Mandeville, "Forty Fabulous Years of Barbie," *Doll Reader,* February 1999, vol. 27, no. 2, p. 42.

58. Kitturah B. Westenhouser, *The Story of the Barbie Doll.* Paducah, KY: Collector Books, 1999, p. 20.

Chapter 6: Lonnie G. Johnson: Super Soaker Inventor

59. Quoted in *Time,* "Soaking in Success," December 4, 2000, p. 108.

60. Quoted in Susan Karlin, "From Squirts to Hertz," Spectrum Careers. www.spectrum.ieee.org.

61. Quoted in *Associated Press,* "Sometimes It Does Take a Rocket Scientist," February 13, 1999.

62. Quoted in *Time,* "Soaking in Success."

63. Quoted in Karlin, "From Squirts to Hertz."

64. Quoted in Vernon Brabham, "'Accidental' Invention Makes a Big Splash," *Inventor's Digest,* March/April 1995, p. 10.

65. Quoted in Michael Klein, "Rocket Scientist/Super Soaker Inventor Turns Propulsion Science into Big Bucks," *Philadelphia Inquirer,* August 5, 1998.

66. Quoted in William J. Broad, "Rocket Science Served Up Soggy," *New York Times,* July 29, 1998, p. 7.

67. Quoted in iSoaker.com, "History of the Super Soaker," June 8, 2000. www.isoaker.com.

68. Quoted in Christy Oglesby, "Innovators Who Break Barriers," February 9, 2001, www.CNNfyi.com.

69. Quoted in *Associated Press,* "Rocket Scientist Behind High-Tech Water Gun Line," November 16, 1998.

70. Quoted in Klein, "Rocket Scientist/Super Soaker Inventor."

71. Quoted in Oglesby, "Innovators Who Break Barriers."

72. Quoted in Johnson Research & Development (company profile). http://johnsonrd.com.

73. Quoted in Oglesby, "Innovators Who Break Barriers."

74. Quoted in Caryne Brown, "Making Money Making Toys," *Black Enterprise,* November 1993, p. 68.

FOR FURTHER READING

Books

Linda Jacobs Altman, *Women Inventors*. New York: NY: Facts On File, 1997. Profiles of interesting women inventors, including Ruth Handler.

Fred M.B. Amram, *African-American Inventors: Lonnie Johnson, Frederick McKinley Jones, Marjorie Stewart Joyner, Elijah McCoy, Garrett Augustus Morgan*. Mankato: Capstone Press, 1996. Lists outstanding African American inventors and their successes.

Jean F. Blashfield, *Women Inventors*. Minneapolis, Capstone Press, 1996. Contains short profiles of women inventors and their creations, including Ruth Handler and the Barbie doll.

Doug Gelbert, *So Who the Heck Was Oscar Mayer? The Real People Behind Those Brand Names*. New York: Barricade Books, 1996. Profiles of people behind the creations of some of our most famous name brand goods.

Laura S. Jeffrey, *Great American Businesswomen*. Berkeley Heights, NJ: Enslow, 1996. Profiles of interesting women who succeeded in the business world. Includes information on Ruth Handler.

Bobbie Kalman and David Schimpky, *Old-Time Toys*. New York: Crabtree, 1995. An interesting look back at the different types of toys children played with in the nineteenth century.

Constance Eileen King, *The Encyclopedia of Toys*. New York: Crown, 1978. A comprehensive look at toys from the eighteenth, nineteenth, and twentieth centuries.

Andrew McClary, *Toys with Nine Lives: A Social History of American Toys*. North Haven, CT: Linnet Books, 1997. A history of how toys changed and developed in our society. Profiles favorite toys such as Erector sets and LEGO bricks.

Anne Mountfield, *Looking Back at Leisure*. Needham, MA: Schoolhouse Press, 1988. Describes the different types of leisure activities in our society throughout history, including information on toys and games.

Robin Langley Sommer, *"I Had One of Those": Toys of Our Generation*. New York: Crescent Books, 1992. A nostalgic look at classic toys and games from the 1950s and 1960s. Includes information on Barbie, LEGO bricks, Erector, Lionel trains, and Milton Bradley.

The Ultimate LEGO Book. New York: DK Publishing, 1999. A glimpse into all aspects of LEGO bricks. Includes many fascinating facts about the toy and its creator. Contains many colorful photographs.

Henry Wiencek, *The World of LEGO Toys.* New York: Harry N. Abrams, 1987. A comprehensive look at Ole Kirk Christiansen and the history of LEGO bricks. Includes photographs and building instructions.

Don Wulffson, *TOYS! Amazing Stories Behind Some Great Inventions.* New York: Henry Holt, 2000. Chronicles the interesting stories behind the creation of a variety of toys and games, including LEGO bricks and Lionel trains.

Websites

Barbie Through the Years (http://web.info-gallery.com). This site chronicles Barbie's history with a timeline from her debut in 1959 to the present.

Milton Bradley (www.quadrangle.org). A brief profile of Milton Bradley's life and accomplishments, including a photograph.

Cool LEGO Site of the Week (www.lugnet.com). Highlights amazing creations made from LEGO building bricks.

Dr. Toy's Guide on the Internet (www.drtoy.com). Contains a variety of information and links to toy histories, best toys, books, stores, articles, and news about toys.

A.C. Gilbert's Discovery Village (www.acgilbert.org). The online site for a nonprofit children's museum in Salem, Oregon.

A.C. Gilbert Heritage Society (www.acghs.org). For serious Erector set fans of all ages.

Gilbert Family Photographs (http://frontiernet.net). Personal photographs from the Gilbert family album.

History of the Super Soaker (www.isoaker.com). Highlights of Lonnie G. Johnson's invention of the famous water gun.

The History of Toys (http://inventors.about.com). Profiles and interesting facts and stories about famous toy inventors and their creations.

Johnson Research and Development (http://johnsonrd.com). Profile and information on Lonnie G. Johnson's company.

Lionel Trains (www.lionel.com). Official website of the Lionel Company featuring the history and background of the company and tips and advice in getting started collecting and setting up electric trains.

Mattel Toy Company (www.mattel.com). Information on the Mattel Toy Company and their products.

Toy Industry Hall of Fame (www.toy-tia.org). This site is categorized by a timeline and contains profiles of individuals who made significant contributions to the toy industry.

WORKS CONSULTED

Books

Roy P. Basler, *Abraham Lincoln: His Speeches and Writings.* New York: World, 1946. A reference book including speeches by Abraham Lincoln with analytical comments and notes by the author. Also included are essays written by Lincoln and his correspondence, including the letter by Grace Bedell and his reply to her.

Billy Boy, *Barbie: Her Life and Times and the New Theater of Fashion.* New York: Crown, 1987. A lighthearted look at Barbie and her impact on the fashion world with her extensive wardrobe.

Milton Bradley Company, *Milton Bradley: A Successful Man.* Springfield, MA: Milton Bradley, 1910. Published in 1910, this book chronicles the life of Milton Bradley and contains personal remembrances and tributes from people who knew him. A glimpse at his life, interests, and passions.

Pierce Carlson, *Toy Trains: A History.* New York: Harper & Row, 1986. A fascinating account of the history of toy trains and the companies around the world that manufacture them. Includes information on Lionel trains and how they compare with and differ from other toy trains.

Gary Cross, *Kids' Stuff: Toys and the Changing World of American Childhood.* Cambridge: Harvard University Press, 1997. A serious and thought-provoking look at the impact of toys on children and their place in our society.

Alan Farnham, *Forbes Great Success Stories: Twelve Tales of Victory Wrested from Defeat.* New York: John Wiley & Sons, 2000. Looks at the stories behind successful businessmen and women. Includes information on Ruth Handler.

Joseph J. Fucini and Suzy Fucini, *Entrepreneurs: The Men and Women Behind Famous Brand Names and How They Made It.* Boston: G.K. Hall, 1985. A profile of famous entrepreneurs and the stories behind their success. Includes information on Joshua Lionel Cowen and his company.

A.C. Gilbert with Marshall McClintock, *The Man Who Lives in Paradise.* New York: Rinehart & Company, 1954. A.C. Gilbert's autobiography. An interesting look at the man behind Erector sets and a variety of science toys.

Elliot Handler, *The Impossible Is Really Possible.* New York: Newcomen Society of North America, 1968. A speech given by Elliot

Handler detailing the creation of the Mattel Company from a home-based business to an international success.

Ruth Handler with Jacqueline Shannon, *Dream Doll: The Ruth Handler Story*. Stamford, CT: Longmeadow Press, 1994. A fascinating first-person account of the creation of the Barbie doll, the business world viewed through the eyes of a successful woman, and Handler's battle with and triumph over breast cancer.

Ron Hollander, *All Aboard! The Story of Joshua Lionel Cowen and His Lionel Train Company*. New York: Workman, 2000. A comprehensive look at the history and background of Cowen. Details the rise of the Lionel Company, including advertisements and photographs of trains and accessories.

Marvin Kaye, *The Story of Monopoly, Silly Putty, Bingo, Twister, Frisbee, Scrabble, Et Cetera*. New York: Stein and Day, 1973. Follows the creation of some of the best-known toys and games in our society.

M.G. Lord, *Forever Barbie: The Unauthorized Biography of a Real Doll*. New York: William Morrow, 1994. Chronicles Barbie's life as if she were a real fashion model.

G. Wayne Miller, *Toy Wars: The Epic Struggle Between G.I. Joe, Barbie, and the Companies That Make Them*. New York: Times Books, 1998. A comprehensive, in-depth look into the complex world of toy making as a big business. Details the triumphs and setbacks of advertising campaigns, new toy designs, and the competitive nature of the business.

Allan W. Miller, *Getting Started with Lionel Trains*. Iola, WI: Krause, 2001. A guide for toy train enthusiasts and hobbyists to get them started with a collection and train setup. Includes background information about the Lionel Company.

Peter H. Riddle, *America's Standard Gauge Electric Trains: Their History and Operation, Including a Collector's Guide to Current Values*. Norfolk, VA: Antique Trader Books, 1998. Written for the serious toy train collector and hobbyist. Includes detailed information on rare trains and accessories of interest to collectors and antique dealers.

Harry L. Rinker, *Collector's Guide to Toys, Games, and Puzzles*. Radnor, PA: Wallace-Homestead, 1991. Details the history of toys and games. Includes tips for toy collectors and many photographs of rare and antique toys and games.

James J. Shea, *It's All in the Game*. New York: G.P. Putnam's Sons, 1960. A tribute to Milton Bradley and his accomplishments both in creating games and amusements for families and in his devotion to the education of children. Includes fascinating personal stories about Bradley.

Bruce Watson, *The Man Who Changed How Boys and Toys Were Made.* New York: Viking, 2002. A comprehensive and fascinating look at the life and inventions of A.C. Gilbert. Includes photographs.

Kitturah B. Westenhouser, *The Story of the Barbie Doll.* Paducah, KY: Collector Books, 1999. A comprehensive guide to Barbie dolls and Barbie doll collecting. Contains information about Ruth Handler's struggles to get the doll manufactured.

Bruce Whitehill, *Games: American Boxed Games and Their Makers, 1822–1992.* Radnor, PA: Wallace-Homestead, 1992. A fascinating, in-depth look at the history of board games, social aspects of games, and tips for serious collectors. Includes information on game makers including Milton Bradley.

Periodicals

Susan Adams, "Boy Toy," *Forbes,* November 11, 2002.

Associated Press, "Rocket Scientist Behind High-Tech Water Gun Line," November 16, 1998.

Associated Press, "Sometimes It Does Take a Rocket Scientist," February, 13, 1999.

Vernon Brabham, "'Accidental' Invention Makes a Big Splash," *Inventor's Digest,* March/April 1995.

William J. Broad, "Rocket Science Served Up Soggy," *New York Times,* July 29, 1998.

Caryne Brown, "Making Money Making Toys," *Black Enterprise,* November 1993.

Michael Klein, "Rocket Scientist/Super Soaker Inventor Turns Propulsion Science into Big Bucks," *Philadelphia Inquirer,* August 5, 1998.

Glenn A. Mandeville, "Forty Fabulous Years of Barbie," *Doll Reader,* February 1999.

James M. Schmidt, "Yesterday's Toy Becomes Tomorrow's Trade," *Today's Chemist at Work,* September 2000.

Maynard Good Stoddard, "The Toy That Built a Town," *Saturday Evening Post,* October 1984.

Time, "Soaking in Success," December 4, 2000.

Internet Sources

Christine Chen, "LEGO Toys Named 'Product of the Century,'" *Business Wire,* December 2, 1999. www.businesswire.com. Brief article about LEGO bricks being named "Product of the Century."

Eli Whitney Museum, "A.C. Gilbert." www.eliwhitney.org. Brief profile of A.C. Gilbert and his Erector sets.

isoaker.com, "History of the Super Soaker," June 8, 2000. www.isoaker.com. The story behind Lonnie G. Johnson's creation of the Super Soaker. Contains technical information and photographs of different models of the water guns.

Johnson Research & Development (company profile). http://johnsonrd.com. History of the company founded by Lonnie G. Johnson. Includes the company's mission statement, fact sheet, and goals for the future.

Susan Karlin, "From Squirts to Hertz," Spectrum Careers. www.spectrum.ieee.org. Brief article about Lonnie Johnson and how he created his Super Soaker.

Christy Ogelsby, "Innovators Who Break Barriers," February 9, 2001. www.CNNfyi.com. Brief profiles of interesting and innovative African Americans, including information on Lonnie G. Johnson.

Salem Oregon Online History Project, "A.C. Gilbert," December 2002. http://salemhistory.net. Contains information about A.C. Gilbert's life and the creation of the Erector set. Includes photographs.

Mathias Tugores, "Legoland," *Sojourn Online*, December 1999. www.sojournonline.com. Photographs and descriptions of a few of the models on display at LEGOLAND.

Wendy Woloson, "Legos," St. James Encyclopedia of Pop Culture. www.findarticles.com. Brief article about Ole Kirk Christiansen and the creation of LEGO building bricks.

A.C. Gilbert Company
  chemistry sets of, 48–50
  Erector sets of, 42–46
  during World War I, 46–47
advertising
  by A.C. Gilbert Company,
    44
  by Lionel Manufacturing
    Company, 30, 32–35
  by Mattel, 72–74
  television, 72–74
Atomic Energy Lab, 50
Aunt Hulda's Courtship, 20

Bailey, Henry Turner, 22
Baker, Newton D., 47
Barbie doll, 8–9, 74–77
Battleship, 24
Bedell, Grace, 16
Billund Woodworking and
  Carpentry Shop, 53–54
board games, 14–15, 23–24
Bonanno, Joseph, 32
Bowles, Samuel, 15
Bradley, Ellen, 22
Bradley, Milton
  board games invented by,
    15, 23
  croquet sets of, 17–18
  early career of, 11–14
  early life of, 11
  importance of play to, 8
  interest of, in early
    education, 21–22
  later years of, 22–23
  lithography interest of,
    13–14

marriages of, 15, 22
Myrioptican of, 20
photos of Lincoln by,
  15–16
promotion of game playing
  by, 16–17
puzzles of, 18–19
Zoetrope (Wheel of Life)
  of, 20, 21
see also Milton Bradley
  Company
Bradley, Vilona, 13, 15, 20
Buffalo Bill, 22–23
building toys
  Erector sets, 42–46
  LEGO, 57–66
Burp Gun, 72, 73

Candyland, 24
Carlson, Pierce, 29
Carson, Johnny, 89
Checkered Game of Life, The,
  15, 16–17
chemistry sets, 48–50
Chen, Christine, 60
children
  development of, 8
  early education of, 21–22
  importance of play to, 48
Christiansen, Ole Kirk
  carpentry career of, 51–55
  community spirit of, 52–53
  early life of, 51
  insistence on quality by,
    61–63
  LEGO created by, 57–66
  religious faith of, 54

tragedies suffered by, 54
wooden toys made by,
    55–57
Christmas
    Lionel trains at, 34–35
    during World War I, 47–48
Chutes and Ladders, 24
Civil War, game playing
    during, 16–17
construction kits, 42–46
Cowen, Cecelia, 28, 34
Cowen, Joshua Lionel
    early life of, 25–27
    inventions of, 26–28
    later years of, 35–37
    marriages of, 28, 35
    photography interest of, 35
    train sets of, 28–35
Cowen, Lillian Appel, 35
croquet, 17–18
Cross, Gary, 37, 41, 65
Cushman, Oliver E., 11–12

Daisy Company, 88
Davis, Al, 89

Eaton, Vilona. See Bradley,
    Vilona
Erector sets, 42–46

flashlight, 26
Four-Minute Men, 46
freon, 85
Froebel, Friedrich Wilhelm
    August, 21–22
Fucini, Joseph, 26

Galileo (space probe), 85
game playing

Milton Bradley's promotion
    of, 16–17
Puritan view of, 15, 16
Games for the Soldiers, 16
Giaimo, Charles, 32
Gilbert, Alfred Carlton
    chemistry sets developed by,
        48–50
    early life of, 38–41
    education of, 40–41
    Erector sets of, 42–46
    inventions of, 50
    later years of, 50
    as magician, 39–40, 41
    Olympic career of, 40
    during World War I, 46–48
Gilbert, Mary, 41, 48
Gilbert Atomic Energy Lab,
    50
Gilbert Institute of Erector
    Engineering, 45–46
girls, train sets for, 35
Grant, Harry C., 27
Great Depression, 30–31,
    54–55
Greenwald, Louie, 67, 71
Greenwald, Sarah, 67, 71
guns
    toy, 72
    water, 85–90

Handler, Elliot
    criminal charges faced by,
        79–80
    Mattel and, 8, 69–72
Handler, Ruth
    ambitions of, 67–69
    Barbie doll and, 74–77
    breast prosthesis created by,
        80

cancer of, 77–78, 80
criminal charges faced by,
    79–80
death of, 80
early life of, 67–69
initial rejection of, 8–9
Mattel and, 69–77
work ethic of, 67
see also Mattel
Help for Ungraded Schools
(Milton Bradley), 22
Herman, Lillian Appel. *See*
    Cowen, Lillian Appel
Hermann the Great, 40
Hollander, Ron, 30, 35
Houdini, Harry, 41
Hubert, Conrad, 26

Indre Mission, 54
Ingersoll, Robert, 28
Intertech, 88

Johnson, Charlotte, 75
Johnson, Lonnie G.
    ambitions of, 82–83
    early life of, 81–83
    engineering career of,
        83–85
    initial rejection of, 9, 86–88
    inventions of, 90–93
    Nerf and, 91
    research laboratory of,
        91–92
    as role model, 93–94
    Super Soaker of, 85–90,
        92–94
Johnson, Robert Treat, 50
Johnson Research &
    Development, 91–92

Ken doll, 77, 78
Kerion, 23
kindergarten, 22
Kindergarten News
    (magazine), 22
Kindergarten Review
    (magazine), 22
Klein, Michael, 91

Lady Lionel, 35
Larami Corporation, 89
LEGO
    creation of, 57–61
    creativity and, 65–66
    quality, 61–63
LEGOLAND parks, 66
leisure activities, changing
    attitudes toward, 8
Liberman, Cecelia. *See*
    Cowen, Cecelia
Life, 23
Lilli doll, 74
Lincoln, Abraham, 15–16, 17
Lionel Manufacturing
    Company
    advertising campaigns of,
        30, 32–35
    catalogs of, 29
    creation of, 27–28
    racing car sets by, 36
    train sets produced by,
        28–35
lithography, 13–14

magic tricks, 41
Massey, Peyton, 80
Matson, Harold "Matt," 69,
    71
Mattel
    Barbie doll and, 74–77

creation of, 69–71
diversification by, 78–79
Mickey Mouse Club, The, and, 72–74
musical toys by, 71–72
problems faced by, 78–80
toys created at, 71–72
see also Handler, Ruth
Metaframe, 78–79
Mickey Mouse, 31–32
Mickey Mouse Circus Train, 32
Mickey Mouse Club, The (TV series), 72–74
Miller, Allan, 29, 35
Milton Bradley Company
early success of, 16–17
economic struggles of, 19
games produced by, 23–24
success of, 20
see also Bradley, Milton
M-1000 (train), 31, 32
Monopoly, 24
Mosko, Ida, 67
Mosko, Jacob, 67
Mosko, Ruth. *See* Handler, Ruth
moving pictures, 20, 21
musical toys, 71–72
Myrioptican, 20
Mystic Fifteen Puzzle, The, 18–19
Mysto Manufacturing Company, 41, 43
Myung, Song, 89

Nearly Me breast prosthesis, 80
Nerf, 91

Oglesby, Christy, 91

Operation, 24

Paradise of Childhood (Froebel), 22
patents, 12, 86
Peabody, Elizabeth, 21–22
Petrie, John, 41, 43
plastic toys, 58–59, 69
play, early attitudes toward, 8
puzzles, 18–19

racing car sets, 36
railroad industry, 30–31
Rinker, Harry L., 10
Ruthton, 80
Ryan, Jack, 74

Schmidt, James M., 50
science kits, 48–50
Shea, James J., 12
Stoddard, Maynard Good, 52
Super Soaker
creation of, 85–86
initial rejection of, 9, 86–88
popularity of, 89–90, 92–94

Tapley, George, 14, 22, 23
television commercials, 72–74
Terrible Fifteen Puzzle, The, 18–19
Thayer, Ellen. *See* Bradley, Ellen
Thompson, Mary. *See* Gilbert, Mary
3-D photos, 35
Toy Building, 71
toy guns, 72
toy making industry
beginnings of, 8

competitive nature of, 71
modern, 10
originality in, 10
toys
  building, 42–46, 57–66
  educational, 48–50
  first, 8
  musical, 71–72
  train sets, 28–35
  uses of, 10
  war, 29–30
train sets
  Christmas trees and, 34–35
  for girls, 35
  Lionel, 28–35
  whistles of, 32
Tugores, Mathias, 63
Turco, 79
Twister, 24

Uke-a-Doodle, 72

Union Games, The, 16
Union Pacific Railroad, 31

Walt Disney Company,
  31–32
war toys, 29–30
water guns, 85–90
Watson, Bruce, 50
Westenhouser, Kitturah, 80
Wheel of Life (Zoetrope), 20,
  21
Whitehill, Bruce, 15, 16
Wiebe, Edward, 21
Woloson, Wendy, 59
World War I, 29–30, 46–47
World War II, 69

yo-yo fad, 57–58

Zoetrope (Wheel of Life), 20,
  21

ABOUT THE AUTHOR

Linda Skeers writes both nonfiction and fiction for children and young adults. She lives in the Midwest with her husband, two sons, and four cats. In her spare time she enjoys reading, camping, fishing, and playing pool.